Taken

ROSIE LEWIS

An abandoned baby.

Separated from her only family.

Searching for a true home.

HARPER
element

Certain details in this story, including names, places and dates, have been changed to protect the family's privacy.

HarperCollins PUBLISHERS
Since 1817

HarperElement
An imprint of HarperCollins*Publishers*
1 London Bridge Street
London SE1 9GF

www.harpercollins.co.uk

First published by HarperElement 2017

1 3 5 7 9 10 8 6 4 2

A catalogue record of this book is available from the British Library

PB ISBN 978-0-00-811301-8
EB ISBN 978-0-00-811302-5

Printed and bound in Great Britain by
Clays Ltd, St Ives plc

Taken

By the same author

Helpless (e-short)

Trapped

A Small Boy's Cry (e-short)

Two More Sleeps (e-short)

Betrayed

Unexpected (e-short)

Torn

Chapter One

Mothers steered their buggies around the orange barricades, small wheels snagging on the rumpled pavement. The low hum of overheating motors filled the heavy air and behind me someone tooted their horn. Squinting against the plumes of dust, I watched a couple stepping out from the taxi in front of me, others ambling hand-in-hand towards the shops. On any other day I might have escaped the clattering of jackhammers and taken refuge down one of the sloping side streets, among the flower stalls and earthy cafés.

As it was though, I didn't mind being stuck behind the wheel. Browsing the central courtyard for samples of cedarwood and patchouli oil while street entertainers played the crowds was one of our most favourite weekend pursuits, but not nearly tempting enough to compete with the experience that lay ahead.

It was a clear morning in mid-July 2011 and my Fiat was rolling slowly towards Queen Charlotte's Hospital in the city centre where Megan, a baby girl, was being cared for by midwives. Born with a cleft palate three days earlier, Megan had been surrendered into the care of social services by her birth mother under a Section 20 voluntary order and, as a foster carer, I had been asked to begin daily visits to the special care baby unit with a view to bringing the newborn home as soon as she was well enough.

Peggy, Megan's social worker, was also responsible for another child in my care – Zadie, a 13-year-old girl who had been staying with us since May. Quiet and helpful, Zadie had begun to relax in her new home and, though I still had a few concerns about her, I was fairly confident that taking on another foster child wouldn't undermine the fragile trust growing between us. When Peggy told me about Megan though, there was a moment's hesitation before I agreed to become her foster carer.

Having looked after little ones before, I knew how easily love could creep into your heart, stealthily taking you by surprise while your mind was distracted with other things. I also knew how painful it could be to say goodbye to children who had carved their own unique place in your family. Tess and Harry, young siblings who came to me as babies, had moved onto adoption after almost three years in our family. It had taken many months to adjust to the loss. After they left I told myself that I wasn't suited to fostering tiny ones – it was so hard to let them go – but as the weeks passed the wonder of their early years came back to me.

Gradually the sadness faded, if not into insignificance, then insubstantial enough for me to appreciate what a privilege it had been to be a part of their lives. I knew that if I wanted to continue fostering I had to accept that helping children to move on to permanent placements was a crucial, and perhaps even the most pivotal, part of my role, and when I ran through the handover in my mind, I realised that even though I'd been jelly on the inside as I readied myself to let the siblings go, I had managed to keep my own feelings hidden from them. The handover had been painful, there was no doubt about that, but from the point of view of the little ones, it went very well.

Though I hadn't seen them since the day they left, I had heard through the grapevine that they were doing very well, and slowly my confidence returned. Soon after Tess and Harry came Sarah, a baby born with severe neonatal withdrawal symptoms. Perhaps inevitably, the bonds grew quickly and though Sarah was only with us for a few weeks, parting with her wasn't easy either.

I was honest enough with myself to suspect that moving another baby onto adoption might be painful, but Peggy had assured me that Megan's case was unlikely to drag on – Megan's birth mother, Christina Hardy, was a severely depressed young woman with a substance addiction who seemed unable to stick to any of the treatment programmes she had been referred to. Besides her dependence on illegal drugs, she had recently fled a violent partner and, with no home of her own, was staying in a refuge.

Although Christina wanted to keep Megan, she had agreed to her being fostered to avoid the trauma of a forced separation. Technically, Christina could revoke her agreement to the Section 20 at any time, but in light of her homeless state and drug-dependency issues, she was more than likely aware that social workers would have little trouble obtaining a more formal, interim care order through the courts.

From what Peggy had said, Christina's chances of securing a full parenting assessment were minimal and the social worker was keen to push for a swift resolution of the case so that Megan could be settled quickly into permanence. Having known the social worker for several months, I felt I could trust her word. Initially she came across as a little brisk, but as I got to know her I realised that she was a professional who was happy to go the extra mile for a child in need. I knew that she would do her best for Megan.

As well as having an excellent social worker on the case, a recent review of the family justice system had found that the excessive delays in care proceedings were damaging for looked-after children. According to Peggy, the findings placed renewed pressure on local authorities to resolve cases within six months so that family finding could begin early on in the child's life. I felt certain that I could handle a separation after a relatively short time.

Chapter Two

And so at a little after half past one I climbed the stairs to the third floor of B wing in Queen Charlotte's Hospital, filled with the anticipation that a new placement always roused in me. Though it would be nice to claim it, I had no feeling of foreboding at that time, no sense of the dramatic twists and turns that awaited us in the months to come.

What I could say honestly enough though was that I was struck by a strong sense of recognition as soon as I caught sight of Megan's little face. I'm still not sure how it was even possible, but from that very first moment she felt as familiar to me as all of the veins and tendons on the back of my own hand.

At the reception of the special care baby unit, one of the midwives checked my Bright Heights security pass and gave Peggy a quick call to confirm my identity. After I had washed my hands and used the alcohol rub to cleanse them, the nurse showed me into the unit and guided me to Megan's crib. Several of the other mothers gave me curious glances as I went, but I was so excited to see the baby that I only half-registered them.

Swaddled snugly in a white cellular blanket, Megan lay on her side in a see-through Perspex open incubator, a folded blanket tucked behind her back to prevent her from rolling over. As I neared, the first thing I noticed was her dark, downy hair. Long for a newborn, it emerged from beneath the white woollen hat she wore in soft wisps, falling across the tops of her ear and towards the nape of her neck. Her delicately fine fringe brushed her eyebrows and skimmed the tips of dark lashes.

Taking in her rounded forehead, flattened nose and large hazel eyes, I felt a rush of tenderness, so much so that my eyes misted over and a lump rose in my throat. She looked so beautiful and vulnerable and, rocked by the strength of my feelings, I'm ashamed to say that, for a split-second, I considered calling Peggy to tell her I had made a mistake – I wasn't sure I was up to caring and then parting with another baby.

'Adorable isn't she?' the midwife whispered. About fortyish, she slipped her arm around my waist as she stood beside me, giving me a friendly, unexpected hug. The tip of a name badge was visible over the top of the plastic apron she wore, fixed to her royal-blue uniform. When she released her grip and turned to face me, I could just about make out the letters: 'ANGIE'. 'We've barely taken our eyes off her since she came in,' she added.

I smiled, knowing that babies in care were often singled out by midwives for their most special attention: the empty visitors' chair at the side of the crib a poignant reminder of their aloneness in the world. 'Absolutely,' I said, all thoughts of fleeing put firmly aside. I loved being a foster carer and my whole family adored looking after little ones. Saying goodbye was tough, of course it was, but I had managed it several times before and there were hundreds, if not thousands, of people all over the country who would snap up the chance of caring for a newborn baby. I was lucky enough to be in a position to take that opportunity. And besides, nothing worthwhile was ever going to be a piece of cake.

'Ready for a cuddle?' the midwife asked, one eyebrow cocked.

'I thought you'd never ask.' I cast my shoulder bag aside on the empty chair beside the crib and rubbed my hands together as if they needed warming up. They didn't – if the inside of my car had turned into a sauna, the hushed, airless interior of the unit felt like a kiln.

'Here she is,' Angie said, planting the tiny baby in my arms. Megan registered the change with a blink of surprise. After several longer, slower blinks she fixed me with an unfocused but slightly amused gaze, as if she'd been expecting me and was wondering why I had taken so long to arrive.

A floating sensation ran through my limbs, the feeling spreading up my torso and fanning itself out inside my chest. I stood transfixed, aware of her warmth seeping into my arms. Edging backwards until my calves touched the back of the chair, I lowered myself down, ignoring the bulk of my bag pressing against the base of my spine.

Angie reached over and grabbed the bag, tucking it on the floor beneath the crib. I thanked her without looking up and shuffled back in my seat, my eyes taking in the tiny purplish veins running in minuscule branches across Megan's cheeks and the slightly mottled skin covering the soft contour of her forehead.

Her button nose was slightly squashed against one cheek and, beneath the small fist hovering an inch from her face, I noticed a cute little pleat in her chin. Just above, her tiny mouth pulsated at intervals around a small medical-looking dummy. It was only then that I took in the small gap, maybe a centimetre or so wide, visible in her top lip. Tilting my head, I tried to see how large an area was affected by the cleft – as far as I could make out, without removing her dummy, it wasn't nearly as extensive as I had feared when I had spoken to Peggy on the telephone. 'I've seen worse,' Angie said, picking up on my scrutiny. 'She'll need surgery in a few months, but if she's lucky she might get away with just one or two procedures.'

'Oh, that's good,' I answered absently, my heart skipping as I touched Megan's small hand. Tranquil and pale, she fixed her gaze on me and closed her fingers tightly around one of mine, almost as if she was claiming me. 'She seems very contented,' I managed to say, though I was so absorbed that my voice sounded muted, even to my own ears.

'That's the baby methadone doing its work,' Angie murmured, leaning close. 'She had another dose a couple of hours ago.'

I looked up sharply. Peggy had mentioned that Megan's mother had a history of drug and alcohol abuse, but somehow I hadn't processed the possibility that she might have used during her pregnancy. I wasn't sure why it hadn't occurred to me – I had cared for babies suffering from neonatal abstinence syndrome, or NAS, before – but I think it was probably because I found it difficult to believe that any drug had the potency to override a mother's instinct to protect. I knew from caring for Sarah that babies were only prescribed methadone if their withdrawal symptoms were particularly severe. In most cases, TLC and a heavy helping of stamina were enough to nurse them through the worst of it. Angie pouted grimly and I pulled a face back. 'Oh dear, poor thing.' And then another thought occurred to me. 'Is that what caused –?' I tilted my head towards Megan, indicating the cleft.

Angie whistled softly. She crossed one leg behind the other, leaned her elbow on the crib and put her other hand on her hip. 'It's hard to say. Some drugs are linked to clefts – diazepam for instance – but as far as we know Mum wasn't on that.' The midwife was speaking so quietly that I had to lean forward to make out her words. 'Christina swore she wasn't on anything. Sister realised little one was clucking the day after she was born. We couldn't leave her to muddle through, poor little love, not without a bit of help. She was in a lot of pain.' And then, with sudden vehemence, she added in a fierce whisper: 'In the States they recognise unborns as victims, so I'm told, but over here we don't seem to see them as people in their own right. Personally I'd prosecute these mothers. We're told not to stigmatise them; that they're the victims and they need help, but most of the time they don't even want to stop. They must know how awful it feels to go cold turkey, but that doesn't stop them putting their own baby through it.' Angie lowered her voice still further. 'And we're supposed to feel sympathy for them?' She blew out her lips. 'Look at the harm they do.'

Quietly enraged, spots of pink appeared on Angie's cheeks. I pressed my lips together, shaking my head. Her words had reminded me of something I learned recently when I attended a local-authority-run course on drug and alcohol addiction. According to the tutor, roughly 1,500 babies a year were born addicted to drugs in the UK, and the figure was rising year on year. What really surprised me, though, was that some remained in the care of their mothers, despite their ongoing addiction.

While I had seen some birth parents battle against the grip that illegal substances held over them, plenty of others seemed to indulge themselves without troubling their consciences too much. Working at the sharp end in one of the largest cities in the UK, I imagined that Angie's view had been coloured by the number of babies she had seen suffering as a result of their mothers' addiction.

Angie ran a hand across her forehead and blew out some air. 'Anyway, what can you do except deal with the fall-out as best as you can? The good news is that baby's coping well on the minimum dose and we're stretching it out to six-hourly now. She'll be on eight-hourly by tomorrow and hopefully off a few days after that.'

'How long before I can take her home?'

Angie smiled then, the vestiges of anger leaving her face. 'Oh, that's wonderful to hear. Lovely to know she'll be going home to a family.' She tilted her head. 'Do you have your own children?'

'Yes, Emily's 16, Jamie's just 13 and we've got another girl staying with us at the moment who's almost 14. They can't wait to meet this little one,' I said, which was mostly true. Emily and Jamie were really excited to have another baby in the house but Zadie had seemed nonplussed when I broke the news about Megan.

Last night Emily and Jamie had delighted in helping me to order a cot, pram and all the accessories online, but Zadie had hidden herself away in her room. I suspected that she was worried about being sidelined with the arrival of another child but I was sure she would warm to the idea when she realised her fears were unfounded.

'That's great, really great,' Angie said, and I was surprised to see her eyes filling up. 'Oh heck, look at me. We grow close to them here, you know. It's surprising how quickly it happens when Mum only has limited contact.'

I threw my eyes up to the ceiling and then gave her a sympathetic smile. 'Yes, tell me about it.'

'God, I'd make a terrible foster carer.' Angie leaned closer and laughed conspiratorially. 'They'd find me half-way across Europe with the baby stuffed inside my coat or something. Angie Wickens, wanted by Interpol! I can see it now.'

I laughed along with her, trying not to jog around too much because Megan's eyelids were beginning to droop. 'I don't let myself think about the end until I have to.'

'Oh,' Angie said, fanning her eyes with her hand. 'It gets me, just thinking about it.' She bit down on her lower lip, looking at Megan thoughtfully. 'We won't discharge her until she's off the medication. Methadone can suppress breathing so she'll need close monitoring all the while she's on that – but as soon as she's off it you can take her home. She'll be at the hospital for her surgery, but she'll come back here for outpatient check-ups. She's only 5lb so they'll want to monitor that, but she's doing well, considering. Feeding can be a bit tricky but don't worry, I'll show you what to do.' She stilled for a moment and then tapped my arm. 'Tell you what, she's due a bottle soon. We try to time her feeds between doses, when she's not too sleepy but not too fretful either. Give me two ticks.'

A few minutes later the midwife returned armed with a bottle of milk and a plastic pipette with a rubber bulb on the end, similar in appearance to the ones I had seen gardeners use to feed plants. Noticing my puzzled stare, she tucked the bottle under one arm and held the pipette out to me with her free hand. 'It's a bulb suction,' she explained. 'You use it if milk pools in her nose when she's feeding.' She must have noticed the look on my face because she quickly added: 'Don't worry – it sounds worse than it is. We won't send her home until you're confident about what you're doing. There's lots of support if you find it tough. I'll give you all the contacts before you leave.'

Angie handed the bottle to me and then gently pinched Megan's toes to rouse her. The baby's eyelids fluttered and then she snorted a half-yawn, half-cough. Her dummy fell out, rolling over the blanket and out of sight. 'Keep her fairly upright,' Angie said, coming around the back of the chair and leaning over the top so that her arms were free to guide me. 'That's it. Now, reach round with what I call your embracing hand, the one you're cuddling her with, and hold her lips together with your fingers. There,' Angie said encouragingly as I touched the teat to Megan's lips. 'You want a tight seal to create some suction.'

Megan's mouth fell open and she shook her head, rooting. 'Make sure you position the teat over her tongue,' Angie said, pressing down gently on Megan's chin. 'The bottle has soft sides so you can squeeze them if she doesn't seem to be getting much, but we've found she can suck effectively if you get the seal right. The cross-cut teats help.' Latching onto the teat, Megan began sucking sleepily. At first there was a random slurping noise, a bit like the sound of a dog lapping at a puddle, and I could tell that it was a bit unproductive. 'Don't be afraid to be a bit more forceful. Unless you fix a seal she won't get much milk,' Angie said, placing her hand on my forearm.

'I'm worried I'll hurt her.'

'You won't. She's a lot tougher than she looks, honestly.'

It was a tricky manoeuvre, and at the back of my mind I was wary of letting her suck too hard in case she choked, but after a couple of attempts I relaxed and got the hang of it. I couldn't help smiling at the loud clicking noises she made as her tongue worked at the teat and then the cute little goya-goya of her swallows. She sucked with a sort of desperation, as if she knew she was going to have to fight harder than the other babies on the ward, the ones with parents close by.

Rivulets of milk ran from her nose down to her chin. Angie tucked a folded muslin square in the fold of her neck, reassuring me that leakage was normal with cleft babies. 'Perfect,' she said, patting my arm. But a minute or so later Megan jerked back, eyes widened in alarm. She fixed a panicked gaze directly on me as if to say, *Please, DO SOMETHING!* 'Here you go,' Angie said briskly, pressing the suction into my hand. With quickening pulse, I worked to clear her nasal passage while she floundered in my arms. It was a relief to find that the suction did its job quickly. Instinctively I shifted the baby to an upright position, making a pillow of my shoulder. After a few rattling breaths she gave a sigh, the curve of her back moulding itself magically into my palm. My heart melted. 'That was great, Rosie, well done.'

I let out a breath and rolled my eyes. 'Phew! That was a bit hairy.'

'It is at first, I know, but you'll get used to it,' Angie said, as Megan began to complain. I set her on my lap again and offered her some more milk, keeping the suction close by on the arm of the chair. Megan pounced eagerly on the teat and Angie gave a little laugh. After a minute or so, she patted my shoulder and bustled off to the nurses' station in the middle of the ward.

Knowing that I wasn't causing Megan any discomfort, it was easier to fix a seal the second time around. Every so often she opened her eyes and gazed up at me, the look so trusting that my heart swelled. Time stalled and, immersed in what I was doing, I didn't notice anyone approaching until a shadow fell across Megan's face. I turned, taking in a pair of pink slippers. I looked up, the swollen but slightly deflated stomach belonging to the woman in front of me revealing that she was one of the newly delivered mothers.

'Hi,' she whispered, introducing herself as Erin. She smiled down at Megan. 'Ah, bless, what a darling.' Her eyes swept over Megan's face, lingering on my fingers as they held the cleft together and the soft-sided bottle. Her brow furrowed inquisitively. 'I can't tell you how glad I am you're here,' she said after a short pause, leaning forward so that her face was level with mine. 'My heart bleeds when she cries. She goes on and on, till she's hoarse. We can't bear it. She even whimpers in her sleep.' Erin pouted her lower lip in a gesture of sadness and frowned. 'Then all of a sudden she goes still, just staring up at the ceiling and you don't hear a peep out of her. It's like she's given up, as if she knows no one's coming.'

The methadone, I thought, glancing down at Megan, though of course, I didn't say anything. She had stopped sucking and dropped off to sleep again, her soft breaths rattling in her chest. 'I came over to give her a cuddle yesterday but' – Erin rolled her eyes sideways in the direction of the nurses' station then lowered her voice to a whisper – 'I got told off. It's not allowed apparently, but I can't bear it, seeing her so upset and all alone.'

'Don't the nurses see to her when she frets?'

'Oh yes, don't get me wrong, they're brilliant in here. They do their best but sometimes there's no one free to pick her up. They're so busy. That's what I said to them – I don't mind giving her a cuddle when my little one's asleep, I said – but it's against the rules and regulations and God knows what else. You know what these places are like.'

My stomach clenched at the thought of Megan's cries being ignored. I held her a little closer after that, tilting her towards me so that her heart was next to mine. Through the tinted windows of the unit, the bright clear sky was subdued in dusty shades of pale blue and grey.

From my position in the low chair there was no view of the road and the only reminder of the city centre was the persistent hum of traffic and the faded shadow of inky buildings set against the sky. With Megan's gentle warmth pressed against my chest and the hypnotic clicking noise as she began sucking again, the city streets fell away into a different realm, vague and irrelevant.

Chapter Three

Barely five minutes later the peace was shattered by a series of howls and loud bangs coming from outside the unit. Turning sharply towards the glass security doors and the reception beyond, I must have jogged the bottle because Megan suddenly spluttered and began to choke again. Silently cursing myself and fumbling for the suction, the commotion going on behind me instantly faded.

I did my best to clear Megan's airway quickly, only vaguely aware of Angie rushing across the ward, another nurse following hastily behind. As her breathing settled I snatched another glance over my shoulder, wondering what on earth was going on.

It was difficult to see anything beyond a blur of royal-blue uniforms, but from the nurses' frantic movements and strained voices of forced calm, I could tell they were concerned. Perhaps sensing something, Megan began to cry. I got to my feet and soothed her, rocking gently from foot to foot. Thankfully she brought up some wind as I rubbed her back, and as soon as she'd quietened I settled her into her crib and popped her a fresh dummy back in. It was just as well I had because at that moment a midwife I didn't recognise hurried over. 'Mum's outside,' she said in a rush, reaching for my bag and handing it to me. 'She's insistent that it's her time for contact so you'd best leave. We'll take the staff exit.'

With a regretful glance Megan's way, I followed the nurse past several other incubators, the tiny babies inside surrounded by a tangle of wires and tubes. Their parents, seated protectively nearby, stared between me and the commotion going on beyond the doors with shocked astonishment.

The further away from Megan I got, the more aware I became of the gritty, surprisingly deep voice of her mother. Almost at the other end of the ward, I couldn't resist another glance behind and saw the face of a small woman somewhere in her early twenties pressed up against the glass doors, her hands resting either side of her like giant suction pads. Dressed in blue tracksuit bottoms and a loose white t-shirt, she had light, thin hair and a narrow face with bloated, heavily hooded eyes. She was flanked by two nurses, each trying to peel her hands away. 'Get off o' me!' she bellowed, her words punctuated by a rattling buzz as she lunged out and jabbed at the intercom. 'Why you letting some stranger hold my daughter? She's *my* fucking baby. *Mine*.'

Despite her aggression, her expression was distraught and when a thread of uncertainty entered her voice, so that she began to sound more upset than angry, I felt an unwelcome trickle of sympathy for her.

'This way,' the midwife said with a curt nod, flinging the door open and ushering me through. Sweeping through a set of double doors, the nurse turned right and then took a sharp left along a narrow, less brightly lit corridor. When we reached another flight of stairs she stopped and faced me. 'We're going to have to speak to the social worker before you visit again,' she said, sounding apologetic but brisk. 'I don't know what they can do about it, but she's going nuts up there. We can't let that happen again.'

After the sterility of the unit, it was lovely to get home to the scent of coffee and the pancakes Emily was making in the kitchen. She downed the whisk she was holding as soon as she realised I was back. 'Tell me, tell me!' she said, waving her hands so that little puffs of flour rose, speckling her rosy cheeks and settling in her dark-blonde hair. 'What's she like? Did you take some photos?'

'Sorry, Ems. I didn't get a chance.'

Her face fell. 'Oh, why not?'

'Photos?' my mother said, coming into the kitchen. Mum was my back-up carer – after attending a course for respite carers she had been interviewed by my fostering agency, who had also checked her background to make sure she was responsible enough to take care of the children I fostered when I was unable to, and had child-proofed her home to pass the local authority health and safety standards check – and had come over to babysit while I went to visit Megan.

My son, Jamie, loped in closely behind, listening to his iPod. With earphones in place, there was that vacant, slightly sleepy look on his face that teenagers so often wore. I slipped a finger behind one of the thin dangling wires hanging from his ears and gave it a tug. 'Hey!' he moaned, jerking away, though there was a playful light in his eyes. 'Quit messing with my muse, Mum.'

'Just saying hello,' I said, smiling. Cool aloofness was the attitude he generally aimed for lately but, at just 13, there were still lots of times when it eluded him.

'Show us then,' he said, with as much detachment as he could muster. He leaned in, trying to shoulder Emily to one side.

'Ow, give over, Jamie!' she groaned.

'Sorry, I don't have any piccies,' I said, holding my hands up. 'The visit came to an, um, abrupt end.' I pulled a face and they nodded knowingly. Having fostered a number of children over the last ten years, my family were well aware of the pitfalls as well as the joys of fostering. While I was always careful not to tell them more than they needed to know, out of respect for the child's right to privacy rather than any lack of trust, they had seen enough over the years to reach accurate conclusions of their own.

I spent the next half an hour telling them all about Megan and how lovely she was, all the while aware that Zadie was still shut away in her room. I wanted the teenager to feel as much a part of this new adventure as Emily and Jamie and, still unaware of the real reason for her withdrawal, I made a conscious note to try and include her as much as I could in the coming days.

Her reticence worried me slightly, but it was Megan who was at the forefront of my mind when I went to bed that night. Whenever I thought of her I felt an irresistible itch to get back to the hospital – I just couldn't wait to hold her again.

Chapter Four

It was another week before Megan was able to cope without the methadone. Her cot was set up beside my bed, the newly purchased sleep suits were all freshly washed and folded, and a steriliser filled with bottles and teats ordered from a specialist supplier over the internet sat unplugged on the kitchen worktop next to the kettle. We were excited for her to join the family, but the midwives had reported that she was frequently uncomfortable and, according to Angie, feeding remained a challenge. There was also some concern that, due to frequent vomiting, she might fail to thrive. She had already lost two ounces since birth so in some ways it was a relief to know that she was in the hands of experts and getting the best care possible, and that when she finally came home, she'd be that little bit more robust.

During the day, whenever Emily and Jamie were at school and my mum was free to spend some time with Zadie, I drove to the hospital and sat in the low chair, alternately feeding and holding her. With small fists tucked beneath her chin she gazed at me as she fed, occasionally stretching out her short arms towards my face. Her cheeks were still red and blotchy; her mother's struggle with addiction leaving its trace on her skin, and often she cried, her knees drawn up to her chest as fierce abdominal cramps gripped hold of her – yet another unwanted legacy from the womb. After each dose of methadone she lay peacefully, gazing ahead with quiet self-possession, but when the drug wore off she screamed herself breathless. I felt awful when mid-afternoon came and I had to leave.

Contact for Megan's birth mother had been arranged for late afternoons to reduce the likelihood of any further upsets, but the midwives had warned me that Christina had a habit of turning up randomly, banging on the security doors and hollering demands to see her daughter. I felt sorry for the nurses; they did their best as stand-in bouncers until hospital security staff showed up, but physical tussles with relatives were way outside the remit of their job. After extracting themselves from the fracas, they then had the task of soothing the other parents on the ward who wished for a gentler introduction to the world for their own babies.

Fortunately there was only one close encounter between us during that first week: Christina climbing the stairs to the third floor as I made my way down. Hands held out in front of her in a position of prayer, as she neared I saw that she was clutching a phone between them, her thumbs running speedily over the keys. When she looked up I slowed my step and steeled myself for introductions, only to find that her eyes drifted over me unseeingly, without a flicker of recognition. Half a second later they fell back to her phone.

I had no idea what she was really like, or how well she handled Megan during her supervised contact sessions, but somehow it was nice to know she was close by, and that there were only a few hours during the day when the chair beside her newborn daughter sat empty.

The day of Megan's planned discharge, the third Sunday in July, was clear and bright. With record high temperatures forecast for midday and no air-con in my old Fiat, I set off early, keen to avoid getting caught in another snarl-up. Mercifully, with only DIY store enthusiasts, football mums and committed members of the National Trust on the roads, the morning traffic was light. By 11 a.m. I had completed the mandatory infant resuscitation course hosted by the hospital and packed the few bits that Christina had bought for Megan in the little *Winnie-the-Pooh* case I'd bought especially for her homecoming. A small white rabbit went in there as well – a gift from Angie, and some beautiful sleep suits that the other parents on the ward had clubbed together to buy.

Midday found us back on the ring road, Queen Charlotte's Hospital shrinking in the rear-view mirror, the precious cargo secured in her car seat beside me. Driving along, I was struck by the number of speed bumps between the city centre and my house, something I rarely noticed before. I cringed every time we went over one, holding myself stiff as if the effort would somehow lessen the impact on Megan's tiny form. She seemed unconcerned though, alternately dozing and then staring with curiosity around the car, tongue darting out through her parted lips.

There was a welcoming committee waiting at the door when we got home, Emily clasping and unclasping her hands and Jamie making a poor job of maintaining his cool. There was no sign of Zadie, I noticed, as I walked up the path with the car seat resting in the crook of my arm, which was probably just as well because by that time the baby was shrieking, the skin on her face a deep, blotchy red – not the gentlest way to make a first impression.

My mother was standing behind her grandchildren. Shorter than both of them, all I could see of her was an arm resting on each of their shoulders. 'Oh, look at the little love,' she said reverentially, peering around Emily's shoulder.

'Me first!' Emily trilled, on her knees in front of the car seat as soon as it touched the floor. Carefully, almost in slow motion, she released the wide straps and laid them gently to one side before reaching in and lifting Megan out. I resisted the temptation to offer any advice; the mother of one of her school friends recently came by a perimenopausal surprise of her own and Emily had been over to babysit quite a few times in the last few weeks. She knew what she was doing well enough.

With Megan secure in her arms she turned away and walked slowly into the living room, the three of us an eager entourage behind. We spent the next hour passing the blanketed bundle between us, already enchanted. When it was Jamie's turn to hold her he sat with rigid arms and scrunched shoulders, as if she were made of the most delicate silk.

Sometimes it took time to encompass foster children into our home and feel completely at ease around them, but we seemed to mould ourselves easily around the under-fives, I suppose because our family dynamics remained largely unchanged.

Chapter Five

What with visits from Peggy, the community midwife and our health visitor, plus an unexpected dash to Accident and Emergency one night after Megan suffered convulsions (a frightening but rare symptom of withdrawal) the next few days alternated between frenzied activity and dazed sleeplessness.

The jarring cries of a newborn were such a foreign sound in our house that when I woke during Megan's first night at home, I lay still and staring into the darkness, thinking that perhaps foxes were getting acquainted outside my bedroom window, or that next door's cat lay injured somewhere nearby.

I knew that babies born with substance addiction sometimes suffered a range of health problems, and Megan seemed to have more than her fair share – if anything about neonatal abstinence syndrome could ever be described as fair. Violent stomach cramps left her crying piteously for hours at a time, interspersed with bouts of vomiting and diarrhoea, and then periods of the jitters, when her hands, legs, and even her lips trembled. Clammy to the touch, her chest rose and fell at alarming speed and when I sat still with her in my arms, I could feel her body vibrating, almost like a toy that was running low on batteries. If I placed my hand flat on her tummy her insides trembled against my palm, something that caused my heart to lurch.

The emergency doctor suspected that reflux was partly responsible for her frequent vomiting and prescribed Infant Gaviscon, an antacid in powder form that was to be added to her formula milk. The thickened feed was more likely to stay down, so he said, but he told me that I shouldn't expect her symptoms to disappear overnight.

He explained that Megan's system was overwrought and advised swaddling her tightly and handling her as little as possible. The less stimulation the better, he recommended, but it wasn't advice that sat easily with either of us. In truth, there were a handful of occasions in that first testing week when I felt I would go mad if I didn't have a few moments to myself. Almost at the end of my tether, I tried placing her firmly in her cot and walking away, but I didn't get far. After a few minutes of pacing the hall, trying to block out the noise, her hoarse screams always drew me back. At least when she was in my arms I felt I was doing something to alleviate her discomfort, and when I picked her up her small body would sag in relief, though she often continued to fret.

Our nights were worse, each a feat of endurance sliced into short, disorientating segments where I got little and Megan got poor-quality sleep. If I tucked her up in her crib she bellowed with a desperation that seemed, in those disconcerting early morning hours, life threatening in its intensity. On more than one occasion, gripped by unadulterated fear, I called the on-duty midwives at Queen Charlotte's Hospital to make sure I wasn't ignoring dangerous symptoms that needed urgent medical care – I'm still grateful for their unending patience and generous reassurances.

My mother, a woman capable of giving the researchers at GCHQ a run for their money, scoured online forums on Mumsnet and Netmums in search of a solution, producing and printing off a detailed list of suggestions for me to try. I worked my way through all of them, and then varying combinations of each, though nothing worked better than a good old-fashioned cuddle.

After the first few nights I got used to snatching a few moments of sleep sitting upright, with Megan's contorting tummy pressed against my chest and her lips quivering against my neck. She still fretted, but it was a soothed, soft whimper rather than a full-on assault on the ears.

As the days went on and the last of the methadone wore off, her cries escalated to shrill, agonising screams. She loved her dummy, sucking on it with furious gusto, but even that didn't stop her crying. Whenever she was out of my arms she grew frantic; in her pram and car seat, strapped in the sloped seat of a supermarket trolley. Sweeping around the shops at speed, I tossed whatever I needed quickly into the trolley with barely more than a glance and then raced into the street again, desperate to offer her the comfort of a hug.

In desperation I bought one of those all-singing, all-dancing bouncy chairs, the ones that some mothers swore by, their newborns whiling away many a contented hour swinging to and fro. Megan was having none of it though, not even for two minutes while I attempted a solo visit to the bathroom.

One of my most successful purchases was a baby sling, and for much of the day I kept Megan strapped close to my chest as I pottered around. After a few hours my shoulders felt like they didn't belong to me, but at least my arms were free to get on with other essential tasks, like eating.

There were days when the tiredness didn't affect me much, and others when my mind was so vague that even making up Megan's bottles seemed like a cryptic puzzle that was beyond me. I can remember standing at the kitchen worktop on at least two occasions and losing count as I scooped the powdered formula milk into carefully measured amounts of boiled water, so that I had to tip the rogue mixture away, sterilise all six bottles and start all over again.

Apart from all the crying, her cleft meant that feeding seemed to take for ever. With barely two hours in between bottles, day trips were not as easy as they might have been, especially as she was frequently sick afterwards. Our health visitor reassured me that, while it may have seemed as if Megan brought up the entire feed, enough probably stayed inside to nourish her.

I had always loved the school holidays but I was glad that Emily and Jamie were both tied up with their own projects during the first couple of weeks of the summer break – Emily had taken a voluntary job at our local hospital, lining up songs for the DJ running the children's radio channel, and Jamie had started working towards his Duke of Edinburgh Award. If he wasn't on the football pitch practising new skills, he was at his friend's house, learning riffs on an electric guitar. When they were home they didn't seem to mind Megan fretting as I worried they might, always offering to take a turn in walking her around.

There were some rare peaceful moments as well. Sometimes during the late evening the cramps relaxed their grip on Megan and she would stare around at us in wonder, as if seeing us for the first time. Emily and Jamie delighted in those times, whispering softly as they dipped their faces to her neck, nuzzling her gently with their chins. Whenever she was out of her room, which wasn't much during Megan's early weeks, Zadie would watch her with quiet intensity, an anguished look on her face. I wondered again whether she felt pushed out, but when I tried to include her or even spoke about Megan, she would lose colour in her face and fly back to her room. I considered the possibility that Zadie was disturbed by Megan's cleft, but she loved to watch those graphic fly-on-the-wall medical documentaries that made my stomach flip over, so I knew she wasn't squeamish like me.

Anyway, Zadie had seemed unsettled by the mere idea of a baby in the house, even before the placement had begun.

* * *

When Megan had been with us for about five days my mum kindly offered to babysit so that I could take the older children out on their own. We decided to go to the cinema and then on for a meal, and it was lovely to spend some uninterrupted time with them all, but strangely surreal as well. Every so often a mild panic gripped me; that sudden sense that something was amiss. When the film was over I called Mum, who assured me in an insistent (if slightly strained) voice that all was fine, but I could hear Megan's cries in the background and, though I'd been longing for a break from the regime of pacing and feeding, I felt a strong urge to get back to her.

It was late when we finally got home and I was pleased to see that Megan had stopped crying. Stretched out on the sofa in one of her cramp-free moments, she was staring up at Mum's face with avid fascination, her shallow breaths racing with intrigue as Mum clucked and cooed. Suddenly she made a funny whistling noise and we all laughed, Emily and Jamie crouching on the floor to join in the fun. It probably didn't help much towards establishing a day-time/night-time routine, but I went along with the fun and games anyway, aware that this baby's charms were already drawing all of us in.

Chapter Six

A week after Megan's arrival, something happened that arrested our long summer days and, for a while at least, turned them upside down. After an early-morning self-harming incident and a high-speed trip to Accident and Emergency in an ambulance, I was astounded to discover that Zadie was several months pregnant.

Deep down I had known that something was wrong – the feeling had dogged me for weeks – but the news still came as a huge shock, particularly as Zadie was the last teenager I would ever have suspected of engaging in risky behaviour. Devout and introverted, she had struggled to maintain eye contact when she first arrived, and, until recently, had barely spoken above a whisper.

The shock was marginally cushioned by the confirmation that Zadie had been several months pregnant when she arrived (the part of me concerned with holding on to a job I loved relieved that it hadn't happened while she was in my care), but she was so young and vulnerable that it was difficult to imagine her sneaking off to meet someone against her father's wishes. The hideous alternative possibility, that she hadn't had any choice, lurked, unacknowledged, somewhere in the back of my mind.

Driving away from hospital the next morning, guilt washed over me. Zadie had spent ten weeks in my care but hadn't felt able to confide in me – a failing that no foster carer would be keen to admit to. Not only that, but I had overlooked signs that now seemed so obvious, such as her unexplained nausea, frantic exercising, no evidence of monthly periods – I felt such a fool.

My mother had held the fort at home and it was a relief to share some of my fears for Zadie over a cup of tea when I got back. It was only after she'd left that the wider implications of Zadie's pregnancy began to sink in.

Soft mutterings from Megan's carrycot interrupted my thoughts and drew me to the dining room, and as I lifted her up the first thing I realised was that she had slept for a whole hour without crying out in pain. Thrilled at this first sign of progress, I kissed her forehead, her soft skin warm against my lips. Her small splayed fingers moved purposely through the air as I carried her along the hall, her lips moving with such deliberation as she stared up at me that it really felt like she was miming. 'Yes, I know what you're trying to tell me, my love, I know,' I said, smiling down at her. 'Your first comfortable sleep. I'm very happy about that too.'

The living room looked like the storeroom in the basement of a shockingly disorganised branch of a baby-merchandising retailer. Apart from all the usual baby equipment, there were baby gifts dotted all around the room; a pink and white blanket crocheted by my mother, a pile of assorted furry and velour soft toys and fluffy blankets from our neighbours all along the street, and a small pink kitten from Peggy.

I was just contemplating the arrival of a second baby in the house and all the associated regalia that might entail, when another thought struck me – what if Peggy decided, when she heard the news, that two babies and a teenager was too much for one foster carer to cope with? Might she worry that my attention would be too thinly stretched? If that was the case, there was a chance that, on the basis of 'last-in, first-out', Megan might be moved on to another foster carer.

A fair number of the foster carers at Bright Heights Fostering Agency operated a strict 'no babies' policy, but there were plenty of others who loved caring for newborns.

I lowered Megan onto her padded mat and gently removed her wet nappy. Her legs were still so thin and scrawny that I couldn't wait to tuck them back into her sleep suit, for fear they might break. As I dabbed her bottom with damp cotton wool, my eyes fixed on the stump of an umbilical cord clinging stubbornly to her tummy. It was sad to think of any baby being parted from their mother so soon after birth. I felt a pang in my chest at the prospect of Megan going through yet another separation so early on in her life.

Chapter Seven

When Zadie came home the next day she broke down and told me the whole horrific story – she had fled the family home to escape her abusive elder brother, and by then she was already three months pregnant. After talking to me she fell into an exhausted sleep and, with Megan asleep in her carrycot, I took the opportunity to email a report to Peggy while the disclosure was still fresh in my mind.

Foster carers are encouraged to keep detailed and accurate notes because, in some cases, their records are summoned by the courts to form part of the case for the prosecution in any criminal trial. I force myself to listen passively if a child makes a disclosure, however strong the temptation to elicit more information from them. Most children possess a strong desire to please and so, if they're asked a question more than once, there's always a risk that they might alter their answer in the mistaken belief that they haven't said what the adult wants to hear. In that way, well-meaning carers asking intrusive questions can influence a child's testimony, thereby prejudicing the case.

Peggy called after breakfast the next morning, shock and concern audible in her tone. Her voice had that slightly echoey quality created by activating the loudspeaker mode and instinctively I lowered my voice, feeling slightly self-conscious. We discussed Zadie and the prospect of her continuing with the pregnancy and then I took a deep breath. 'What about Megan?'

'No change as far as I'm concerned,' Peggy said in that definite, no negotiation tone of hers. 'I can't think of a better way for Zadie to learn about caring for a baby than watching someone she trusts do it, can you?'

Relieved, I leaned against the wall and loosened my grip on the cord of the telephone. It sprang out of my hand and vibrated against the receiver. 'No, no, I can't. Thanks, Peggy,' I added after a moment, slightly worried that I'd been worrying in the first place. I was well aware that I needed to keep myself in check, striking the right balance between giving Megan everything she needed, everything she deserved, and all the while bearing in mind that our time together was limited.

'Anyway, if things go to plan Megan might have moved on to adopters by then.'

'Great,' I said, pleased that Peggy was still committed to keeping to tight timescales in Megan's case. There was no doubt that making the transition from foster to forever family early on in her life would help to minimise any lasting sense of trauma and loss – we were often told in training that separating a child from their main caregiver could have profound effects, interfering with their development and the quality of all of their future intimate relationships as well as impacting on their self-esteem, social skills and long-term mental health – and, infinitely less important but nonetheless also present in the back of my mind, it would be easier for all of us to let her go. 'Now, before I forget, Megan's LAC review is scheduled for tomorrow at ten. I'll need you there obviously.'

'Tomorrow?!' I cried, exasperated. 'That's a bit late notice to arrange cover, isn't it?' Looked after children, or LAC, reviews were meetings held at regular intervals during a child's time in care to discuss their care plan and keep everyone involved in looking after them – the child's parents, their foster carers, school or nursery teachers, health professionals and, in certain circumstances, police officers – updated in terms of their progress and any difficulties they may be experiencing. In other circumstances I would have been happy for Emily to babysit while I popped out, but local authority rules dictated that looked after children must only be cared for by registered back-up carers with a minimum age restriction of 18.

Peggy tutted. 'Well, you'll just have to bring the children along if you can't organise something in time.' There was a crackle on the line and a shuffling of papers. I pictured the social worker tapping urgent notes in a Word document using one finger on the keyboard and motioning silent, stern commands to the administration staff around her with the other.

A whirlwind character, Peggy never held back from speaking her mind and I had heard on the grapevine that her blunt honesty had put one or two noses out of joint in her office, particularly those of the senior management. Despite being sent on repeated diversity and equality training refresher days, she refused to toe the party line simply to keep her bosses happy, steadfastly sticking to her strongly held views.

Once, so I'm told, she brought her dog into the office for a week when he was unwell, in direct defiance of instructions from above. Through closed doors, in the middle of a heated 'discussion' with one of her line managers, Peggy was overheard to say, 'I haven't taken a day off sick in ten years, not a single one, which is more than I can say for you lily-livered lot with your stress vacations and mini-breakdowns. Now, either Pug stays and I work, or I'm taking unpaid leave until he's better. It's up to you.' Despite misgivings, the manager caved in and Pug spent the week resting in his basket underneath Peggy's desk.

One of the joys of working with someone like Peggy was that you could say exactly what you thought and she never took offence, although you had to be prepared to hear her own opinions pointed out in no uncertain terms. I had often thought that if Alan Sugar ever needed a replacement sidekick to keep a stern eye on the applicants in *The Apprentice*, Peggy would have been his ideal woman.

'Someone here can watch them for an hour if needs be but it's not very convenient. I'd rather you made other arrangements.'

Chapter Eight

As it was, I didn't have to bring the children along. Emily and Jamie were both out with their dad for the day and my mother was more than happy for me to drop Megan and Zadie over to her while I went. The LAC review was to be held in one of the interview rooms at the local authority municipal buildings and Peggy was waiting in reception when I arrived. Solidly built, with steely grey hair and heavy-framed glasses, she angled her chin when she saw me, a greeting I had come to accept as friendly, though until I drew closer and she smiled, it looked anything but.

Des, my supervising social worker from Bright Heights Fostering Agency, usually accompanied me to LAC reviews but plans were in place for him to transfer to the US to conduct research into a youth scheme that was working well there. With a mountain of paperwork to catch up on before he left, he had sent me a text to say that he wasn't sure whether he'd make it to the meeting.

Apart from the statutory visit each month that he was obliged to make, I had heard very little from him in the past weeks, although he had paid us a flying visit in the week, to meet Megan. Having developed a close friendship with him since becoming a foster carer, I missed his impromptu visits and calls.

Angie, the midwife who had overseen Megan's care in hospital, was standing at Peggy's side. She held her arms out when she saw me and after giving me a hug the first thing she wanted to know was how Megan was doing. I was about to tell her when Peggy said, 'Shall we get on, ladies?' She rammed the thick file she was holding under her arm and turned, marching wheezily in the direction of the lifts. Angie raised an eyebrow and we exchanged smirks, like chastised schoolgirls, before falling into step behind. 'Christina's not here yet but we'll go ahead without her,' Peggy said as the lift moved towards the second floor. I had been feeling a bit nervous about meeting Megan's birth mum after witnessing her volatility at the hospital and so was quite relieved to hear that. 'The morning'll run away with us otherwise and I've got far too much to do.'

The interview room was tiny, so small that it was a struggle to open the door wide enough to get inside. A long table took up the entire width of the space, leaving no gap at either end to access the mismatched chairs on the opposite side. The chairperson, a thin man in his early forties with a well-manicured beard and coppery, thinning hair, was already seated in one of the nearest chairs. Standing awkwardly in the cramped quarters, he shook our hands and introduced himself as John Noble.

'It was the only room free, sorry, everyone,' Peggy said, her voice booming off the walls. 'Now, I would climb over there, but I'm not sure I'd ever make it out again. At least, not without a hoist.'

'It's all right, I'll go,' I offered, pleased that I was wearing trousers. I perched on the desk and swung my legs over the other side, taking a seat on one of the unforgiving wooden chairs. Angie followed my lead and sat beside me. Peggy thanked us, taking one of the seats opposite with a loud humph. John retook the seat beside Peggy and glanced at his watch. It was almost ten o'clock, the time the meeting was scheduled to begin.

'Christina's not here,' Peggy told John. 'I received a call from the legal team earlier, which I'll tell you about in a moment. I suggest we start on time and if she turns up we'll have to recap. Agreed?'

Peggy's tone invited compliance and we all nodded our agreement. John went on to tell us that he was present to mediate between the different parties and ensure the correct procedures were followed, but without Christina present it was unlikely that any disagreements would arise. After introducing ourselves, Angie was invited to give a summary of Megan's health-care needs and I was surprised to hear that there were some concerns about her hearing as well as her low weight.

Apparently, a test conducted in the hospital soon after Megan was born had suggested that there might be some loss of hearing, and the details had been recorded in her red book. While I had skimmed through the log, in truth I had been so focused on dealing with her symptoms of withdrawal that I hadn't taken much notice of anything else. I knew that children with neonatal abstinence syndrome could suffer a range of health, behavioural and learning difficulties, and my heart squeezed at the possibility of little Megan having so much to contend with. I felt a sudden stab of fury towards her birth mother.

Angie must have noticed the unease on my face because she was looking at me when she said: 'Just because we failed to get a clear response from the first hearing test doesn't mean we won't at the next one. It's difficult to test hearing in a baby as young as Megan and the results are certainly not conclusive. We find that, for most, their hearing improves when their cleft is corrected.'

I nodded my thanks to Angie and at John's invitation I summarised Megan's first week at home. I told them that she had been prescribed an antacid and that her sickness had eased a little. 'She's coping well, bless her. I'm beginning to see light at the end of the tunnel.'

Angie tilted her head to one side and gave me a warm smile. After updating them on Megan's routines and general well-being it was Peggy's turn to address the meeting, and what she had to say took us all by surprise. 'Christina was arrested yesterday for shoplifting,' she said, looking at each of us in turn. 'Her probation officer has been in touch with our legal team to say that she's been bailed and was released this morning. Heaven knows where she is now.' The social worker sighed and then looked at Angie. 'I have to say, any suggestion of disability isn't going to help us in tying things up quickly this end. Most adopters run a mile at the mention of health problems.'

Angie held up her hands. 'It's a consideration at this stage, that's all. Megan's head circumference is on the small side but we'd expect that with NAS babies and, as I said, newborn hearing tests aren't conclusive. Megan will need a repeat test in a few weeks to see if the results are the same. If they are, she'll be referred to an audiologist.'

Peggy nodded decisively and then moved on to discuss Megan's care plan. Usually, when a baby is removed from its mother, an assessment is undertaken to establish their ability to parent, but since Christina's drug-dependence problems were so severe, Peggy was almost certain that she would relinquish her parental rights of her own accord.

It was unusual for parents to give up their rights to their children without a fight, in my experience, although it sometimes happened, particularly when they knew in their hearts that they weren't able to care for them. If Christina contested the local authority's plans to permanently remove Megan from her care though, a lengthy legal process would follow, with lots of toing and froing between Christina's representation and the local authority legal team. It wasn't unusual for cases to take anything up to two years or more to resolve, so I was happy to hear Peggy reiterating that she was confident of a speedy resolution.

'We're making efforts to trace Megan's birth father at the moment, which is proving to be more complex than you might think,' Peggy said with a coded glance. 'Christina is insistent that' – she glanced down, consulting her notes – 'Briz Clark, her most recent partner, the one she fled from, isn't Megan's father, although as you probably know, we need to demonstrate to the court that we've exhausted all avenues of enquiry in finding him, whoever he may be, before we rule the option out. Of course, if he's found he may want to be considered to care for Megan, but my guess is that Christina is simply plucking names out of the air and hoping she'll come up trumps. She isn't at all sure who he is.'

Angie inclined her eyebrows meaningfully and blew out some air. After establishing that no one had anything further to add, John proposed a date for the next review and closed the meeting. Angie gathered her belongings and gave me a quick hug. Peggy inclined her head. 'Thank you, Angie,' she said, as the midwife shuffled herself back over the table. 'You too, John.' The chairman shook our hands. I grabbed my bag ready to follow them out but Peggy lifted her hand. 'Rosie, would you stay a moment? I'd like a word if I may –'

John held the door open for Angie and when it was just the two of us left, Peggy asked how Zadie was coping after the shock confirmation of her pregnancy. I had just finished updating her when the door swung open and crashed into the back of Peggy's chair. The social worker's jaw dropped, one of her habitual habits, and she turned around.

Both of us stared at the young woman standing in the doorway.

Chapter Nine

'Fuck, what you doing sitting in a cupboard?' Christina demanded of Peggy in the rich, husky tone I remembered from the hospital. I hadn't noticed it then, but Megan's birth mother was clearly from the Newcastle area; her Geordie accent unmistakable in the confined space.

'I wanted somewhere small enough to contain you in case you flew off the handle again,' Peggy retorted, standing up with a groan and rubbing the small of her back. She tilted the back of her chair and ushered Christina in, the vague twinkle in her eyes the only clue that she wasn't completely serious.

Christina was wearing a short denim skirt, black ankle boots and a closely fitted, low-cut top. She looked so slender that I never would have guessed she'd recently given birth if I hadn't known already. 'What d'you expect?!' she cried, though without the venom I might have expected. There was a degree of warmth in their rapport, suggesting that Peggy and Christina knew each other of old.

After slamming the carrier bag she was holding and a mobile phone with a large glossy screen onto the table, Christina slumped heavily into the nearest seat, sideways on, one elbow hooked over the back. She ran her eyes around the pokey room and sniffed. 'Well, ain't this the dog's bollocks?'

Peggy returned to her own seat. 'Strictly speaking, Christina, this meeting is over.'

Christina scowled and shifted herself around. 'Christ almighty, this chair's hard! Where's the cushions?'

Peggy shook her head and sighed. 'Fucking government,' Christina continued, oblivious to the social worker's stern glare. 'Snatch your kid before the nurse's even stitched up your oo-jah, then can't be arsed to give you proper chairs. Bloody arseholes!' She twisted her legs around, rested her elbows on the top of the carrier bag and fell into conversation with me. 'They took her off me the minute I dropped,' she said in a nasally tone, the skin around her nostrils red and sore, as if she'd blown her nose too much. 'Plain. Fucking. Rude.' Each word was stated with a noisy slap on the table. 'I'm sick to the back teeth of it all, to be honest.'

Peggy's mouth twitched at the corner. She breathed out so that her nostrils flared, and then composed herself. 'Megan needed immediate medical care, Christina. You were told that was likely after your 20-week scan. You jolly well knew what was going to happen and don't pretend otherwise.' I was surprised to see how easily Peggy confronted her and how naturally relaxed she seemed; I guessed that, in her job, being able to construct a dialogue with all sorts of people while challenging them as well was a valuable asset.

'Yeah well, you know you're gonna croak one day, don't mean you're fucking happy about it,' Christina snapped, unfolding her arms and banging her hands down on the table, the rings she wore on each finger jangling against the grey melamine top.

'Christina,' Peggy said with a warning note.

'What? I'm telling it like it is, that's all.' She sniffed again and let her eyes roam the room. Her gaze finally settled on me. 'Who's she anyway?' she asked in a tone that was suddenly perfectly reasonable and serene. She jerked her head in my direction.

'This is Rosie Lewis, Megan's foster carer.'

'Oh right,' she said, looking at me from the corner of her eye now she knew who I was. 'Beautiful, ain't she?' she asked and there was a note of aggression in her tone, as if daring me to disagree. I was used to that and knew better than to expect instant trust when caring for someone else's baby. It was something that grew slowly; each time a parent saw their little one clean and nicely dressed for contact, every time they found fresh nappies and wipes in the bag sent with them, or perhaps a photo addressed to Mummy or Daddy tucked away somewhere for them to find. Trust usually came in time.

I nodded, smiling. 'Absolutely, yes, she's gorgeous.'

Her jawline softened and she turned her face towards me again, leaning closer. 'Ain't nothing wrong with her, 'cept for that gap in her lip and loads of babies have that. I keep telling them she's all right but they don't wanna listen. All babies puke, it ain't just Megan. She's got it a bit worse, probably 'cos of the butter.'

I frowned. Opposite me, Peggy gave a sigh of exasperation.

'What's that face about? I ate a load of butter when I was pregnant. It was like one of them cravings or something. That's what did it.'

'Is that what they're calling it these days?' Peggy mumbled.

Christina cut across the social worker with a contemptuous look, turning her attention back to me. She looked worn out, which wasn't surprising considering she'd recently given birth, but there was sharpness in her face too, in character rather than features. She looked knowing somehow, as if she'd gathered more experience through the years than most other twenty-somethings.

Her brown eyes were red-rimmed and watery, shadowed with heavy greyish pouches, and her irises were bloodshot and dull, as if she hadn't slept in days. In some ways her appearance was a surprise; apart from looking extraordinarily tired and laid low with an apparent heavy cold, she was actually quite attractive, her dark blonde hair fluffy around her face and no trace of the wizened, emaciated look you expect of an addict. Without looking at Peggy she jabbed a thumb fiercely over her shoulder. 'This is the sort of shit I get every time I come here. Nazis, the lot of them. They're all the same. I don't get told nuffink about my own baby. All they do is pick holes all the time.'

'Well, it would help if you'd turn up on time,' Peggy pointed out. 'If you'd arrived at ten when the meeting began you would have heard all about how Megan is doing. We've discussed her care plan, daily routines, contact arrangements,' she said, tapping each one off on her fingers with the forefinger of her other hand. 'I can recap now, if you'd like? You have contact this afternoon as a matter of fact. You'll be hosting, Rosie. I presume that's OK?'

My eyes widened. Peggy had summarised contact times about twenty minutes earlier, but said nothing about me hosting the event. She had also emailed a copy of the contact schedule through to me a few days earlier, but no venue had been stated. 'Uh, I –' I floundered. Since the demand for supervised contact at family centres was high, social workers were often keen for foster carers to cover sessions in their own home, provided there was no threat to their personal safety. Issues surrounding contact were usually discussed at the beginning of a placement, when plans for the child's care were set out by the social worker. Peggy hadn't said a word about it, so I had naturally assumed the contact would go ahead without any involvement from me. It was typical of her to spring the idea on me.

'We're at full capacity our end,' Peggy said firmly. 'We'd appreciate it, Rosie.'

'Of course,' I said, trying not to grimace.

Christina's mobile wobbled and pinged. She swiped at it and then stared down at the screen, her expression going blank. Peggy cleared her throat noisily and pushed a sheet of A4 paper across the table. Christina snatched at it, the scrunching noise as she screwed it up in her palm clearing the glaze from her eyes. She stared at it for a full two minutes and then looked up at Peggy, her expression agog. 'Ten?!' she cried, waving the paper around, although she seemed to be responding to Peggy's earlier comment about the start time of the LAC review. 'I was told eleven, not ten. Who can get anywhere by ten o'clock? What am I, a fucking owl?'

'The rest of us managed to get here punctually,' Peggy said wearily, as if she'd said the same thing time after time. 'And I haven't the faintest idea where you got 11 o'clock from. I sent a letter with the time clearly stated to the manager at your refuge three days ago, along with a voucher to claim back any transport costs. A copy was sent to your solicitor and I also sent you a text-message confirmation, an email and I called your mobile this morning and left a voice message.' Peggy clasped her hands together and rested them on the thick file in front of her. She leaned forward, staring hard at the young woman. 'What else would you have me do, Christina? Arrange for a butler to wake you? Tea, croissants and the morning paper perhaps?'

I sank back, cringing inwardly, though I couldn't help feeling a flash of admiration for Peggy at the same time. It was refreshing to hear her challenging Christina's attempts to shirk responsibility, though I feared the young woman might explode in response. She did colour slightly, but then all she did was give a slow roll of her eyes. 'Yeah, well, people like you don't have to get buses everywhere, do you? You don't have a clue what it's like in the real world. The buses don't run that regular where I am.'

'Twaddle,' Peggy scoffed. Christina stared at her, wide-eyed and adamant, but she didn't say anything in defence. 'It wouldn't have anything to do with the fact that you were only released from police custody this morning, I suppose?'

Christina sniffed briskly, her eyes flicking over to me and then quickly away again. 'Yeah, well, might have been that an' all.' She rolled her shoulders, quickly recovering her dignity. 'I wanted something to wear to the meeting today, didn't I? I need to make a good impression so you give me my baby back. What was I supposed to do? Turn up naked?' She looked back at me, garnering support. I tried to keep my expression non-committal.

Peggy adjusted her glasses and consulted the thick wad of papers in front of her. 'Let's see. Ah yes, here we are. I'm told you stole five pairs of trainers and 19 liquid eyeliners.' She turned back to Christina and fixed her gaze keenly. 'Who exactly were you trying to impress?'

Christina's mouth opened and quickly closed. She examined her nails, which were short and jagged, and then turned back to me. 'Fucking police state, that's what this country is. I might as well pack up and go and live in Russia. Even they don't dish out this sort of crap. In fact I'd go today if it weren't so fucking cold over there. More cameras than rats where I live, there are.'

'Hmmm, evidently,' Peggy snorted. 'A dearth of buses but no shortage of cameras.'

Christina's jaw fell slack. 'What you on about now?' She looked across at me again. 'I only get about half of what comes out of 'er mouth.'

Peggy scratched her short grey hair with sudden vigour. 'All I was trying 'a do was make myself presentable,' Christina continued. 'Make a bit of an effort, you get me? What's wrong with –'

'What you *need* to do is get yourself clean,' Peggy cut in matter-of-factly, whipping her glasses off and waving them in the air to punctuate her point. 'There's no benefit in prancing around in fancy trainers when you're rotting away from the inside out, is there?' Her tone was flat with no room for negotiation and, aside from muttering something crude under her breath, Christina didn't bother trying.

My head was spinning. Christina was antagonistic and outrageous and she seemed to have a completely distorted idea of how the world worked but, in spite of a lingering resentment towards her for the harm she had caused Megan, I actually found myself liking her. I wasn't sure if it was her Geordie accent, which seemed to make the most fearsome people sound friendly, or her complete lack of any artifice, but there was something about her that was genuinely disarming. I shook my head and blinked a couple of times, tuning back into the conversation. '– and we want to secure Megan's future while she's young enough not to know too much about it,' Peggy was saying. 'We know from studies that the sooner babies are settled, the easier –'

'But I love her,' Christina burst out, her lips puckering. Her legs were jiggling up and down so violently that one of her kneecaps hit the table. 'For fuck's sake,' she growled, wincing. 'That's what you lot don't understand. I love her to bits.' The muscles beneath one of her eyes began to twitch. I could tell she was close to tears. 'God, don't you get it? I just wanna hold her without ten thousand people standing around, judging me. It really fucking hurts, all this shit.'

Peggy's expression softened. She sighed, rubbed the inner corners of her eyes with thumb and forefinger then put her glasses back on. 'I don't doubt it, Christina. But love alone can't keep her safe. Megan needs warmth and security and someone calm to take care of her. Someone who's able to put her needs first. You live a rackety life, love, not right for a baby, especially one with additional needs. You know that, deep down, don't you?'

Christina started to cry. It wasn't a howling display designed to garner sympathy but rather a quiet, reluctant release of emotion. Tears trickled down her cheeks and I bowed my head, a lump rising in my throat. Peggy handed her a tissue and she blew her nose loudly. I glanced out of the small window at the end of the room and stared out over the local authority car park, the sound of Christina's quiet sobs moving me more than I would ever have expected or wanted them to. She had harmed a helpless baby and I had strong feelings about that, but viewed dispassionately, there was no malicious intent – it had happened as a by-product of hurting herself. It was such a sorry state of affairs that I couldn't help but feel sad for everyone involved.

'Come on now, don't upset yourself. Let's talk about these referrals you keep ignoring, shall we?' Peggy said, kindness creeping into her tone. 'You're a young girl.

You've got your whole life ahead of you and you're surrounded by people who want to help, love. Let's get you booked in again and –'

'Oh God,' Christina screeched bitterly. She stood and grabbed her carrier bag. One of the plastic handles caught on the back of the chair and she gave a cry of frustration. There was a waft of tobacco as she hauled it free and threw herself at the door. 'I can't hack no more of this shit!' she shouted, in the corridor before Peggy even had a chance to protest. The door banged behind her. I stared at Peggy in surprise.

'Bloody hell,' the social worker said, gathering her papers into a pile and banging one end into a block on the table. 'I could shake her, honestly I could.'

'She won't go for help?'

She sighed loudly, air wheezing in her throat. 'Oh, she goes all right, picks up her methadone and then tops it up with God knows what else when she gets out. She's a character, I'll grant you that. I actually quite like the girl; that's why it's so damn frustrating.' She raised her eyebrows, heaved another sigh and then set her papers down gently, patting the top. 'Anyway, on the bright side, Megan's doing a little better you say?'

I nodded. 'She seems to be a bit more comfortable. The Gaviscon's helping, I think, although she still throws up after every feed.' I gave her a rueful smile. 'She has a knack of catching me right here,' I said, patting my chest, 'no matter which position I hold her in.' Peggy huffed a soft laugh. 'She's sleeping a little easier as well. She really is a gorgeous baby.'

The social worker levelled her gaze. 'Hmmm, yes, she is. And I'm supposed to constantly undermine your relationship with her so that you don't get too attached. It's what we're told to do for our foster carers when they're looking after babies.' She bit her lip thoughtfully. 'Only, if Megan were my own child I'd want you to love her utterly and completely, no holds barred, because the way we're loved as babies defines how much love we'll have in our hearts when we're adults.'

I smiled at her. 'I'll keep her close, don't worry about that.'

'Yes,' she said, looking directly at me. 'I thought as much. But you'll suffer the consequences when she leaves, that's all I will say. And believe me, it's going to hurt you a lot more than it'll hurt anyone else.'

I gave a soft shrug. 'That's as it should be.' I knew that if Emily or Jamie had been taken into care, I would have wanted whoever was looking after them to be smitten, however painful the eventual parting.

Peggy gave me a satisfied nod. 'Well, don't say I didn't warn you. Right, so, contact stands at four times a week for now, as you'd have seen on the schedule I emailed. When we next go to court I'll try and get it reduced. Let me know how it goes this afternoon. If it's too difficult at home we'll try to work something out, but Christina's mild enough. Her bark's worse than her bite.'

'So today's contact is going ahead then?'

Peggy's jaw dropped again so that she gained a severe look. She peered at me over the top of her glasses. 'As far as I know,' she said abruptly. 'Why would you think otherwise?'

'I thought maybe, with Christina's cold and everything, she didn't look well enough to be around a baby and if she's infectious –'

'That's no cold, Rosie,' Peggy scoffed. 'She's been at the snuff, that's all that is. And she's got a touch of sinner's eye, I shouldn't wonder.'

'Sinner's eye?'

Peggy nodded grimly. 'It's one of the places hardened addicts use to inject – the soft tissue around the eye. Either Christina's worked her way through all the veins she can find and it's the only place left, or she's going for the big guns now she's no longer pregnant.'

I blanched; my stomach contracting.

'High impact,' Peggy explained as she pushed her chair back and rose. She winced, her lips clenched together as if in pain. 'Hits the brain faster,' she added a little breathlessly, a few beads of sweat appearing on her brow. 'Gives them the head rush they're looking for.'

I grimaced again and Peggy shook her head, her expression relaxing. 'My goodness, Rosie, you've led a sheltered life,' she said, eyes twinkling with amusement. 'You should do my job for a few months. That'd cure you.' She turned stiffly and held the door open for me. 'By the way, I've got to go into hospital tomorrow so you'll need to contact the fostering team manager if there are any problems while I'm away. I'll be back in the office next week, all being well.'

'Oh, nothing serious, I hope?'

'Something and nothing,' she said briskly, flapping her plump, reddened fingers through the air. She barked a laugh as she followed into the corridor. 'Mind you, if you call the office next week and they tell you I'm dead, you'll know I underestimated the situation.'

I laughed, and then we both went our separate ways.

Chapter Ten

I collected Megan from my mother's house straight after the meeting, but Zadie asked if she could stay for a while longer and help to sort some coloured squares into a pattern for making a patchwork quilt. Mum readily agreed, especially when I told her about Christina coming over for contact. 'Best you stay here,' Mum said, giving Zadie a wink.

I was surprised to see Des waiting on the doorstep when I got home. 'Ach, I'm sorry, Rosie,' he said, as I climbed out of the car. I wondered whether he had been talking to his brothers back in Scotland – his accent was particularly pronounced today. 'I was too late to make the meeting. I thought I'd try and catch you's here.' His hair was wilder than ever, presumably because he'd been rushing, the long curls criss-crossing over themselves across the top of his head, his slightly crumpled trousers and shirt-tails visible beneath the leather jacket he wore lending him a dishevelled glamour that could only ever happen by accident.

In contrast to his appearance, Des gave off an air of indefinable knowing. Nothing ever seemed to faze him or rob him of his calm. No matter what was going on around him, you always got the feeling that he'd been expecting it all along.

'That's OK.' I pulled my handbag up onto my shoulder, closed the driver's door and walked around to the other side of the car, for Megan. Des got there first, chivalrously lifting her seat out for me and holding it easily in one hand. Since finding out that he was leaving, something had changed between us. I wasn't sure what, but I stood awkwardly for a moment, my keys dangling in my hand. Des seemed perfectly comfortable, though, as usual. With his long legs planted wide, he gave a small jerk of his head. 'Coffee, then? Before I head back to the office?'

I nodded, turning towards the house, but he caught hold of my arm with his free hand. 'I thought we's could take a walk, grab something on the way.'

Megan wailed as I secured her into her baby harness, but the noise softened to a whimper as she curled herself up against my chest. With one cheek pressed against my top, she blinked in the sunlight and gave a contented sigh. The air was perfumed with the sweet summery scent of newly cut grass, but in the light breeze I could still smell Megan; her soapy cleanness, and the faint spice of freshly washed linen.

As we walked along, the movement soothed her and she nuzzled further down into her cocoon. I curled my arms around the bulk of her, even though the support wasn't needed, and listened distractedly as Des told me about the foster-carer recruitment drive being initiated by Bright Heights. I think he mentioned something about the agency looking for volunteers to stir up some local interest. Normally I would have been happy to help out, but I was too absorbed by Megan's movements against my chest to take much notice. I found myself concentrating on her tiny, bird-like breaths, making sure that she was getting enough air.

'C'mon,' Des said, when we passed a café. He guided me up the shallow steps with one hand, and then held the door open for us. At the table I loosened the straps of the carrier, but Des insisted on taking Megan so that I could have a rest and drink some tea.

He lifted her out and sat across the table from me, shushing and rocking her when she mewed. I rolled my shoulders, lifted the carrier over my head and let out a long breath. I felt two stone lighter whenever I put Megan down.

Des was a lively character who always seemed to take up so much space, so it was funny to see him metamorphosing in front of my eyes; his big hands arranging Megan's blanket with such gentle attentiveness, his usual booming voice softly controlled. It was at times like that I thought it was a shame he'd never had children of his own. It was easy to imagine him surrounded by adoring, slightly rowdy kids, gales of laughter rippling around their comfortable home.

I smiled involuntarily. It didn't escape his notice. 'Something funny?' he said, lifting his brow. I shook my head, but I couldn't rid myself of the smirk. He didn't comment, but I detected the faint flicker of a smile on his lips, creases of amusement around his eyes.

I started to tell him about the LAC review, but stopped abruptly when the waitress arrived to take our order. Des glanced up at her and made some comment I can't quite remember, but it made her laugh. From that standing start, they very quickly progressed to discussing a joint love of rock music and geometric art. I sat watching them in silent admiration. Des always seemed to fall into easy conversation with people, no matter where he went. It was a gift that never ceased to amaze me.

When the drinks arrived I offered to take Megan back while Des drank his, but she had fallen asleep in his arms and he didn't want to disturb her. I told him more about the meeting and he nodded here and there, but for most of the time he kept his gaze down, fixed on the baby's face. He looked up sharply when I told him about Christina coming over for contact though. 'Why did you's agree to that?' he said, looking annoyed. 'You're under no obligation to host. Ach, it's my fault, I should have been there. I'll call Peggy this afternoon; tell her it's not happening.'

I put my cup down, shook my head. 'No, don't do that. I've agreed to it now. Let's just see how it goes.' Supervising contact was rarely an appealing prospect for foster carers, but there were advantages to holding the sessions at home. Bungled arrangements, overstretched contact supervisors and transport issues meant that sessions held at family centres were often delayed or cancelled.

Hosting the contact at home, as well as providing a relaxed, comfortable environment for what was sometimes a difficult, stressful experience for children, gave foster carers an opportunity to observe and record any changes in their behaviour while their parents were around. In my experience, children found it reassuring to know that the people responsible for caring for them were able to interact positively.

Megan was too young to worry about the politics of it all of course, but staying at home meant that her feeding routine and nap times weren't interrupted, and she wouldn't need ferrying around in unfamiliar cars by a stream of different contact supervisors either.

'Aye, OK, but you call me if you feel you're in over your head, right?' He kept his gaze fixed on me until I nodded, then he looked away, but his heavy brows were still knitted together, his lips set in a stern line. Something about his irritation pleased me, I think because I felt that there was someone looking out for me. I was grateful for his concern.

We left the café in silence, Megan back in place on my chest. We walked on together for maybe 200 yards or so, but then Des stopped. I went on for a pace two before I realised he wasn't beside me. When I turned he said, 'Rosie?'

It seemed as if he were about to ask me something, but our attention was snatched by a whirling buzz as a helicopter passed overhead. We both looked up, watching as its bulk faded to a distant dot and then out of sight. I looked back at him questioningly, but the moment had passed. He took a few brisk strides towards me and went on ahead. I fell into step beside him.

Chapter Eleven

Later that afternoon I awaited Christina's arrival with trepidation. The session had been scheduled for 2 p.m., but the hour came and went with no sign of her. At first I wondered whether she might have had trouble finding our house, but by half past two I decided she probably wasn't coming and got ready to go to the shops. Just as I was about to strap a sleeping Megan into the pram though, I heard a commotion beyond the front door.

I stood in the hall for a moment with Megan in my arms, my head tilted as I tried to work out what was going on outside. The silhouettes of two people were visible through the frosted glass of the door, and from the way they merged, parted, then crossed over again, there seemed to be some sort of scuffle going on between them. Instinctively, I held Megan closer and ducked out of sight, but then I heard loud outbursts of laughter. A few seconds later, the doorbell rang.

'Oh, hello,' I said, my eyes drifting from Christina to the man standing behind her. At least a decade older than her, he was skinny, with a drawn, pale face and bedraggled, shoulder-length hair. 'I'd almost given up on you.' I didn't bother trying to disguise the thread of irritation in my tone.

Christina, who was holding an ice cream, gave me a blank look. Her companion stared at me, equally vacant. After giving her a brief shove in the back, propelling her towards the house, he took a puff of his cigarette, blew a smoke ring in the air and then dropped the stub on the path. I stared at him with incredulity, but neither he nor Christina batted an eyelid, although she jabbed him hard in his chest and threw out one leg, grinding the stub under her shoe.

'You'll have to wait for Christina outside, I'm afraid,' I said, as they readied themselves to come in. I tried to sound as if I wasn't going to brook any argument, although my pulse was beginning to race. Megan stirred in my arms.

'This is Lee,' Christina said, as if she thought that was enough to prove his credentials. 'He's all right.' She was wearing leggings, shoes with extraordinarily high heels and a stringy long-sleeved black top that slipped off one shoulder as she climbed the front step. Once in the hall she took Megan from me without a word and tottered off out of sight. Lee made a move to follow her but I quickly took a step sideways, blocking his way.

'Sorry, Lee. There's a café in the park along the way if you'd like a cuppa while you're waiting.' My pulse quickened again, but I stood firm.

He stared at me for a second or two, shrugged and then craned his head around the doorjamb, his face just a few inches from mine. 'Laters, Chris,' he shouted down the hall, his fusty breath hot on my face. I turned, partly because of the overwhelmingly strong stench of nicotine and stale aftershave, but also to see if I could work out where Christina had taken herself off to. There was no sign of her, but from somewhere downstairs she grunted a noise of acknowledgement.

'Oh, Lee?'

He turned. 'Yeah?'

'Would you mind taking that with you?'

'Huh?'

I nodded towards the path, where faint wisps of smoke were still rising from the half-finished cigarette. He gave me a look that suggested he thought I was the sort of person who kept the food tins lined up in the cupboard in alphabetical order, then trudged over and kicked the butt into the hedge.

In the living room, Christina had kicked off her shoes and was sitting on the sofa, her legs tucked up beneath her. Megan lay sleeping in the curve of her right arm, and in the same hand she held a mobile phone, the back of which was chequered with green and yellow striped tape. One of her thumbs moved swiftly over the screen. With impressive dexterity, she managed intermittent licks of the ice cream she held in her other hand without disturbing Megan or diverting attention from her phone. 'All right?' she said, biting off the bottom of the cone.

'Yes, yes, thanks.' I caught myself staring at her and looked away. I stood for a moment, not quite knowing what to do. Strangely, I felt as if I was intruding, although Christina looked perfectly at home. Still scrolling, she crunched on her mouthful then proceeded to suck ice cream through the hole in the cone. When there was nothing much left to slurp and her efforts grew very noisy, she ran her tongue around the inside the cornet then folded the soggy remains into a bite-sized piece, popping it into her mouth.

It was difficult to strike up a conversation with someone who was so engrossed in other activities. I made several attempts, and Christina made a few noises in response, friendly ones, as far as I could decipher, but nothing substantial enough to build on.

'Megan's likely to wake soon. I think I'll get her milk ready,' I told her. Christina nodded but didn't say anything in reply. Somehow, she'd managed to retrieve a set of small white headphones from one of her pockets and was busy installing one of the earpieces into her ear. A booming beat was audible through the other, which was dangling close to Megan's head.

I hovered on the threshold to the kitchen, wanting to say something, but not sure whether I should. New mothers often resented what they viewed as interference from outsiders and I was reluctant to start our relationship off on the wrong foot. My stomach tightened with the thought of such a loud noise near the baby though, making the decision for me. 'I think that might be a bit loud for little ears, Christina,' I said, as mildly as I could.

Christina didn't seem to mind my interference. Without a change in her expression or a word in reply, she grabbed the earpiece and lodged it into her other ear.

Megan woke up about twenty minutes later, squinting and blinking as her eyes adjusted to the light. Christina noticed. She tilted her arm so that Megan's face was shielded from the glare, then set her phone aside on the sofa. Using her texting hand to hold Megan's lips together, she took the bottle in the hand where her ice cream had been and got on with it. She seemed to be managing well but after taking an ounce or so, Megan began to choke. 'Christ alive!' Christina shouted, thrusting Megan at me. 'I can't stand it when that happens!'

I positioned Megan over my shoulder and patted her gently on her back. I had found that she seemed to be able to clear her own airway when she was upright, and got less distressed than when I used the pipette.

'She all right?' Christina asked. Her face was clouded with concern, and she'd even removed her headphones.

'Yes, she's OK now.'

'Give her back here then,' said Christina, holding out her arms. I sat on the other end of the sofa and watched as Megan took a little more milk, and then Christina cradled her over one shoulder. 'Fucking gorgeous, in't she?'

I smiled. 'She certainly is.'

Next thing I knew, one of the earphones was back in Christina's ear, the other end of the wire attached to a different phone that had somehow materialised, this one smaller than the first. 'Yeah, no, I bloody know!' she shouted. Staring into the middle distance as she spoke, I eventually spotted the tiny microphone on the wire hanging close to her chin. She was engaged in a conversation with someone else.

Megan's head bobbed around on Christina's shoulder as she spoke. I felt a strong urge to go to her, but I forced it down, staring down at my hands instead, and then picking imaginary bobbles from the sofa cushion beside my leg.

'I'm gonna get her back, you know,' she said a few minutes later. I did a double take when I saw her eyes resting on me, unsure at first whether her phone call had ended. 'As soon as I get back on my feet she's coming home with me.'

I nodded, keeping my expression non-committal. From what Peggy had said, there was next to no chance of that, but what happened between Christina and social services was really neither here nor there. My job was to care for Megan and support contact for as long as prescribed. The rest wasn't really any of my business.

'I am, you know.' She was watching me carefully to see if she could detect any sign of disagreement. I didn't say anything either way.

'They're soft shits, most social workers, but they're sneaky with it. Coming out with loads of bilge in them meetings. And, my God, do they love their meetings! All the fucking time, meetings, meetings, fucking meetings. Makes them feel important.' I cringed at Christina's language, relieved that Zadie was still safely out of earshot, at my mum's. I knew that the words meant nothing to Megan, to her they were just harsh sounds, but it still seemed wrong for her to hear them. Still awake, she was resting her cheek against Christina's shoulder, her thumb close to her mouth as she gazed around. 'Try to stitch you up and tie you up in knots they do – that's their game, though Peggy's a bit different. She's all right.' It was ironic, I thought, that she should speak highly of someone like Peggy, who was one of those social workers unlikely to grant her any slack. 'You gotta be wise to their tricks, that's all. I'm gonna show 'em they're wrong about me. Just 'cos I've been inside a few times they've got it in for me. Ain't right, is it?'

I pursed my lips and tilted my head, my eyes widening a touch. Surely she couldn't mean *that* sort of inside? 'Inside?'

She looked at me askance. I realised then that *that* was exactly what she meant. 'Oh-h, I see,' I said, trying not to hyperventilate. 'You mean prison?'

Christina nodded nonchalantly, as if it was an ordinary, everyday comment to pass. 'Yeah, course. There's perks to being inside, but it's when you come out you get all the shit.'

'Perks?' I said faintly. I was still wondering why Peggy hadn't considered Christina's incarceration worthy of a mention.

'Yeah. You get looked after proper, you know? Loads of company and games, that type of thing. And most of the screws are really nice to you. You've got your bastard ones of course, but nah, it's all right.'

My heart softened towards her. 'Do you really mean that?'

She sniffed, angling her free shoulder so that she could wipe her nose on her top. 'Yeah, course. Some's worse than others. The one I was in was done up so it was all right. Some of them are right crap holes, ain't they? You just gotta be lucky.'

I raised my eyebrows. 'I wouldn't know. I'd be interested to see inside one, though not as an inmate,' I added with a wry smile.

'You ain't never seen inside a prison?' Christina almost sounded scandalised, as if I were a Sydney resident who knew nothing of the Opera House. Or a Parisian who thought the Eiffel Tower unworthy of a visit.

I shook my head.

'I ain't got none!' She suddenly burst out, dropping her head back and closing her eyes. She exhaled heavily. 'I told Cooper that. Jesus!' I shook my head, not following, but then I realised that she was talking to someone else again, on what appeared to be yet another mobile phone, the back of this one encrusted with lots of tiny diamantes, and grubby-looking holes where other diamantes had once been. A minute later though, Christina had vacated her rudimentary call and command centre, and Megan was back in my arms. 'Soz, I gotta go. I'll bring some claim forms with me next time, yeah? You could maybe help me with filling them in?'

I nodded. I didn't mind helping, and part of me was sorry that she had to ask someone she barely knew.

'Cheers, babe,' she said, kissing the top of Megan's head and then skidding along the hall. What had caused her to leap up at that precise moment wasn't obvious, but she was clearly in a hurry. Moving at warp-speed, she almost tripped down the front step on her way out.

Chapter Twelve

Gradually the withdrawal symptoms released their grip on Megan and by the time she was five weeks old she was able to get through parts of the day without being held, a blessed relief to my sore back. It was a joy to see her brow no longer continually creased in discomfort, so that she was free to take more notice of the world around her. Most days were warm enough for her to wear only a cotton vest and nappy and during her wakeful periods I settled her on the rug in the conservatory, propped up on soft cushions so that she could watch the leaves dancing on their branches and Jamie darting in and out with his friends. Both Emily and Jamie showered her with attention during these ever-increasing tranquil moments and towards the end of August, when she was almost six weeks old, she rewarded their efforts with her first smile.

It came on one of those glorious summer days when the sun was tamed by just enough cooling breeze to make the 80-degree heat comfortable. Somewhere in the distance a lawnmower droned, the warm air sweetened by the scent of fresh grass and, with a day free of contact and no meetings to attend, we were all able to make the most of spending time together at home.

Megan was nestled in her usual spot, breathlessly captivated by a faint clinking as the long blinds hanging at the patio doors flapped against the frame. I knelt beside her with the intention of changing her nappy but, irresistibly sidetracked, I leaned my face close to hers and began to coo instead. 'Hello, my gorgeous baby,' I said lazily, leaning down and touching my nose to hers. She fastened her gaze on mine, one of her small hands reaching out to grasp a chunk of my hair. 'Ow!' I squealed playfully, easing her hand away. 'What are you doing to Rosie?' I smiled and tickled her tummy. She beamed up at me, her cheeks a dusky pink from the heat, and then suddenly her eyes creased, her misshapen mouth widening into a beautiful, gummy smile. Half a second later it was gone, but not before Emily, Jamie and Zadie had noticed.

'Wow! Did you see that?' Jamie shouted. Emily squealed. Megan's face crumpled, alarmed at the sudden change in our expressions. Zadie, who had been quietly watching, was instantly beside her, whispering words of comfort and taking Megan's small hand into her own. I was bowled over by an immense sense of pride at that moment, which sounds strange, I suppose, since neither Zadie nor Megan were mine, but both of them had been through so much.

After such a difficult start, every milestone felt like a massive achievement, particularly in the light of some slightly worrying news that had emerged the day before. Our health visitor had referred Megan to an audiologist after a follow-up hearing test had thrown up the same results as the earlier one at the hospital. The audiologist told me that she suspected Megan had moderate unilateral hearing loss, meaning that she probably struggled to hear quieter sounds in one ear. There was some hope that the cleft was responsible for a build-up of fluid in the middle ear and that when it was repaired during the second of her scheduled operations at around 18 months old, some hearing would return, but until then it was yet another obstacle Megan had to try to overcome.

At least, I thought, as I watched Emily, Zadie and Jamie making a fuss of her, she had plenty of people around to stimulate her development. Invariably one or the other of us played and spoke to her when she was awake. I hoped that such a lively environment would help her to thrive.

Apart from one statutory visit I heard very little from Des during the summer holidays, and not much from Peggy either. I assumed that the bureaucratic wheels were still in motion and there was no reason to believe otherwise, but in the back of my mind I worried that Megan's case might be one of those left to drag on.

I had never forgotten Tess and Harry's horrified bewilderment when I broke the news that they were going to live with a new family. The siblings had been staying with us for almost three years by the time they were matched with an adoptive family and, though I tried to nurse them gently through the separation, the sense of rejection they felt was painfully evident in our last few days together. It was excruciating to watch them going through it and I desperately hoped that Megan could be spared a similar experience.

Contact continued throughout August, Peggy reassuring me that Christina's past convictions were minor and non-violent. Frustratingly though, there were often times when Christina didn't show up. That didn't worry me too much, since I was home anyway, but on other occasions she'd arrive over an hour late and still expect to come in, her eyes fixed and glossy as she concentrated on holding herself upright.

Standing on the front step with a carefulness particular to back-pain sufferers and the inebriated, she held her limbs stiff and roared with white hot (slightly slurred) fury when I refused to let her in. I felt bad for turning her away, but there was no way it would have been safe for her to carry Megan around when she was that worse for wear. Besides, we often had trips organised and it wasn't fair on the older children to cancel them at the last minute.

After three successive late shows, Peggy intervened and arranged for supervised sessions in one of the family centres belonging to a neighbouring borough, one with free capacity. Surrounded by other members of staff, it was easier for the contact supervisors to refuse late entry to Christina than it was for me at home, and they followed standard protocol, waiting around at the family centre for 20 minutes after the scheduled start time in case of problems with public transport or the like.

In many ways it was a relief to be taken out of the equation but I didn't like sending Megan off with people I didn't know. Contact sessions were often covered by agency contact supervisors, and we rarely saw the same person twice. As well as that, Christina continued to turn up at random times, so Megan was often left in her car seat for long periods at a time, her reputation for projectile vomiting meaning that the contact workers were wary of picking her up. Often she was returned home in a distressed state having spent the entire time strapped into her car seat, watched over by unfamiliar people. Quickly I'd sweep her up to cradle her, my stomach burning with protectiveness.

On other occasions Christina brought friends along with her, one or two, according to the contact supervisors, smelling strongly of alcohol and cigarettes. Peggy soon put a stop to that, insisting that only close relatives were allowed access to Megan. From then on Christina went alone, although once or twice her father, whom she rarely saw, accompanied her.

Whenever Megan went for contact I rushed around the house tidying up, throwing piles of milk-drenched clothes into the machine or sterilising bottles, but within half an hour I was looking forward to scooping her up again. The early months had been a challenge; some days so exhaustingly long that one seemed to merge into the next, but the difficulties only strengthened our bond if anything, and at the back of my mind I was beginning to suspect that I was enjoying caring for her perhaps a little too much.

When the time came to let her go I told myself I would do so to the best of my ability, as I had several times before, but I knew that Peggy was right – saying goodbye was going to hurt. I wasn't worried about myself so much, but I knew that the longer she stayed with us, the deeper her own attachment to us would grow.

Chapter Thirteen

It was in mid-October and Megan was just over three months old when I heard about the first in a series of stumbling blocks on the path to her adoption. We were on our way to hospital for the first corrective operation on her cleft and when we arrived at the station, my mobile rang. Several commuters helped to lift Megan's pram across the wide gap from the train to the platform and, after hurriedly thanking them, I fumbled around in my bag for my phone.

'There in good time then?' Peggy said. Without waiting for an answer she went on to ask who was looking after Emily, Jamie and Zadie while I was away. She could never remember their names, referring to them as 'those others', but it was sweet of her to consider my own children as well as those she was responsible for. It was a small gesture, but one that often meant a lot to foster carers. Megan's lip repair wasn't a complicated operation but required a general anaesthetic and an overnight stay in hospital. I told Peggy that my mother had agreed to spend the night at my house, an arrangement the children were more than happy with – Emily and Jamie had always loved spending time with their grandmother, and Zadie had grown fond of her as well. 'Good. I'll call when my shift ends if you like?'

'Oh no, don't worry,' I said. 'She'll probably be so groggy after the op that she'll just sleep. I'm allowed to stay with her and hopefully we'll be going home first thing tomorrow.'

'Fair enough,' she said, her voice muffled by the rumble of trains and pitchy station announcements coming over the tannoy. 'I'll fill you in now then. There have been some developments.'

'Oh right?'

'We've got our Section 38, as planned. Christina wasn't very happy, as you can imagine, but there we are.' I vaguely remembered Peggy mentioning that a court hearing had been planned for earlier in the week, but foster carers were rarely involved in the legal process so it wasn't something I particularly took a note of. A Section 38, ICO (interim care order) meant that Christina now shared her parental rights with the state. With the Section 20, voluntary care order superseded, she no longer had a right to remove Megan from care.

'Christina's contesting our plans and has insisted on an assessment, I'm afraid, although she's still dropping in and out of her rehab programme, so I've warned her she won't get far. She's proposed her father and his partner as potential guardians for Megan if she's ruled out, so things are looking a little more complicated,' Peggy continued, 'and one of her friends has put herself forward as well.'

My heart sank as I steered the pram, one-handed, through the arched concourse towards the ticket barriers. Megan started when we reached the street, blinking in the bright sunlight. When I leaned over to adjust the parasol and give her some shade, she beamed at me with a gappy-lipped smile. 'They'll all have to go through an initial evaluation with –' Peggy explained, her words fading as a double-decker bus and then a lorry clattered past. I closed my eyes, straining to hear her above the noise from the street. Her voice echoed and became clear again. '– full assessment if they're deemed suitable.' I groaned in acknowledgement. Peggy immediately took me to task.

'You need to keep an open mind, Rosie,' she reminded me sternly. 'Kinship care often works well.' She was right, of course. It wasn't my place to make presumptions on the suitability of people I had never even met, but while going to friends or relatives seemed on the surface to be the next best alternative for children who were unable to live with their birth parents, in reality there were often complications. I knew of several cases where children had left foster care and moved in with their grandparents, only to be taken back by their parents once the radar of social services had shifted its focus onto other targets.

Personally, I could only think of a handful of cases that had worked out well, but I knew that my experience was far more limited than that of Peggy and her colleagues, who likely worked upwards of 30 different cases at a time. 'Christina's given us a few names to work on in the search for Megan's biological father,' Peggy went on. 'We're in the process of testing at the moment. No DNA match as yet, but we're still awaiting results from two. I'll let you know as soon as I hear anything.'

We took a bus to the hospital, Megan sitting on my lap and dazzling the smartly dressed woman next to us with adorable smiles. After a while she grew fidgety so I turned her around to face me and lifted her onto her feet. She loved bearing weight on her legs and swaying with the movement of the bus added to the excitement. She crowed, throwing herself into a bounce with such enthusiasm that her chin collided with my nose. 'Ow!' I shrieked, increasing her delight. She bobbed around again, her breath held as she watched me expectantly. I couldn't resist indulging her and engineered another collision, another overdramatic shriek. She convulsed, her giggles drawing attention from the other passengers. Their doting smiles quickly faded, though, when an arc of milk shot from her mouth and splattered all over my top. There were a few lingering stares, others turning to look avidly out of the window. The woman next to me stiffened, her knee shrinking slowly away from mine.

I was well used to being soaked but still made a little noise of surprise. Megan found the whole event highly funny and choked a fresh wave of gurgling giggles. She never seemed to mind being sick, her mouth snapping closed immediately after the deed as if nothing had happened. For a second or two I just stared at her, floundering. After the tiniest hesitation the woman beside me kindly offered to hold Megan while I changed into a clean top. She smiled warmly at Megan and held out her hands, the string of coos and smile she drew in return giving me the confidence to hand her over. She took her from me with precise care, as if she were a grenade with a faulty valve. I had perfected the art of changing quickly over the weeks and managed it discreetly, even in the confined space.

For the rest of the journey I supported Megan on my lap so that she could look out of the window, her small hands pressed up against the glass. Flashes of green passed by, the central spiked tower of one of the cathedrals visible in the distance. We drove on through a market, fragrant street food and vintage craft on display in the canopied stalls. All around there was vibrancy – crowds of people, conversation and colour – though none of it interested me as much as Megan's response to it. I watched her face as she scanned the shoppers milling around, her eyes flicking rapidly to and fro.

The bus slowed and juddered to a stop. Megan turned to watch as passengers filed along the aisle, the pale skin on her neck momentarily visible before disappearing beneath the folds of her rounded chin. My stomach clenched at the thought of her having an operation – she looked so tiny and vulnerable – but my GP had assured me that the surgeons were among the best in the world. I was confident she was in the safest hands.

As the engine rumbled and the brakes hissed, a cyclist flashed by. The tiny muscles in Megan's cheeks worked furiously and she bobbed on her toes, as if it were the most astonishing sight ever to be seen. And then, as the bus surged forwards to join the traffic, her mouth creased into a random smile that illuminated her whole face. I pressed my cheek against hers and tried to work out what had captured her attention. Her sweet dewy dampness was overlaid by that intangible smell babies have and, with a sudden rush of tenderness, I nuzzled my nose into her neck.

Chapter Fourteen

We reached the hospital a little after 9 a.m. and, having already met the children's surgical team a month ago on the pre-admission visit, we found the place easily. The ward was spotlessly clean with a faint smell of pine, tall painted trees and smiling forest animals stretching its wildlife theme up to the ceiling and in brightly coloured rugs across the floor.

Within an hour we had been seen by the surgeon who would be carrying out Megan's lip repair and nose reshape, and the anaesthetist had introduced himself as well. Megan cooed and smiled at them, crying only when one of the nurses fastened a band around her upper arm and tapped the soft skin inside her elbow, looking for a vein to take some blood. I held her close, keeping one of her arms lodged tightly around my back to stop her wriggling. She struggled and writhed nonetheless, all the while staring up at me in horrified amazement, as if she couldn't believe I was allowing such a travesty to happen. In the end one of the other nurses squeezed a few drops of liquid sugar into her mouth to distract her. It worked a treat. Arrested by the strange but marvellous new taste, Megan stilled, eyes wide with interest.

She was due to go down to theatre at 4 p.m., and so wasn't allowed any more milk after 10 a.m. The hours in between passed slowly, particularly towards mid-afternoon when Megan grew tetchy with hunger. Taunted by the smell of dinner being cooked in the distant kitchens, she threw herself around on my lap, her cries gaining a bit of a growl. I made a seat of my forearm and paced the ward with her facing outwards so that she could see all that was going on, my other arm clasped around her chest. The new position worked well for an hour or so. Visitors passed by, flowers or edible treats clutched in their hands, and whenever they said hello or caught her gaze, her little legs jiggled around in excitement.

As I ventured into the corridors I started to wonder about Christina's father and the friend who wanted to adopt Megan. I knew that their initial assessment would involve local authority and criminal record checks, a process that usually took several weeks. Provided those checks were satisfactory, they might then be allowed to move on to full assessment, a notoriously lengthy process that could take anything from six months to a year to complete.

While the knowledge that so many people wanted her might be a source of comfort to Megan when she was older, I worried about the potential for long delays. I knew that Peggy would do her best to wrap things up quickly, but assessments involved the gathering of information from a number of different people, something that lay outside of her control. But then again, hadn't Peggy said that the guests Christina brought along to contact had smelt strongly of cigarette smoke and alcohol? If that was the case, they wouldn't stand a chance of proceeding to full assessment – social services automatically rejected would-be adopters and foster carers if they had smoked within a year of their application, even if it was only a single cigarette at a party. Sometimes even e-cigarette users were turned down. I felt a flicker of hope at the thought and then swiftly admonished myself for being so ungenerous.

It was only fair that the people closest to Megan's birth mother were given the chance to be considered, even if it meant a delay in placing her with adopters. As a foster carer, it was my job to support the process and manage the consequences in the best way I could. That was the message I kept telling myself anyway, as I paced the colourful corridors.

In the recovery room a few hours later I couldn't take my eyes off Megan as she slept, hardly able to believe the transformation in her appearance. Her nose, no longer leaning to the side, formed a perfect, neat little bump, two tiny nostrils taking the place of the gap that had been there before. A long strip of white medical tape ran the length of her mouth and across her iodine-streaked cheeks, a vertical wound just visible beneath, where the cleft had been.

I leaned over and stroked a few fine tendrils of hair back from her forehead, relieved that, for now, the medical interventions were over and done with and everything had gone to plan. Megan came to with a slow, disorientated blink a minute or so later, her pupils narrowing as she turned her head and looked around. Her eyes widened in alarm as they focused on the unfamiliar room. Her swollen lip quivered.

'Hello, my sweet baby,' I crooned, and as soon as she caught sight of me she relaxed, her expression so trustingly that it clutched at my heart. After a moment she began whimpering, the sound croaky and dry. My stomach twisted with a longing to pick her up and make her feel better. I glanced at the nurse hovering nearby. 'Is she in pain?'

'Hungry, more like,' she said in a thick Liverpudlian accent, patting my arm reassuringly. 'I'll fetch some warm milk.'

Megan was too sore to take her bottle so we fed her using a small syringe. Bleary-eyed, she searched my face questioningly, her lips puckering as if to say, can you believe what happened to me? I dipped some cotton wool into warm water and bathed the iodine from her skin, using cotton buds to clean the creases beneath her eyes. 'All better now, love,' I kept saying, trying to comfort her with a smile. It was so hard to reassure little ones when they were too young to understand what was happening to them. I felt a tightening in my stomach, desperate to reassure her that I had her best interests at heart.

* * *

Back on the ward the lights had been dimmed and I was pleased to see that the nurses, who sat quietly behind their long desk at the far end of the ward, had set up a trundle bed for me beside Megan's cot. The narrow strip of sky visible through the wide windows along one side of the ward had darkened to a deep blue, the streetlights glinting silver over the grey pavements below.

After another dose of pain-relieving medicine Megan became drowsy. I wrapped her in her pink blanket and settled the two of us down on the low bed, shuffling back to lean against the bare wall. I stared down at her as she hovered on the cusp of sleep, listening to the soft whistle of her breaths. The sound of a trolley roused her as it clattered by, her hazel eyes flickering blue as they caught the light. Her lip curled into a sleepy half-smile but the fine crust around the wound cracked, pulling on the soft skin and making her wince. With the tiniest bobbing movement of my arm her small body fell slack and she dozed off again, her mouth dropping open to reveal the dark black stitches inside.

A short time later the ward grew quiet, the distant cries of young babies and the low blur of conversation from their parents fading as they went off to sleep. It had been a long day and as my own eyes began to droop my mind brushed once again over Christina's father, his partner and then her friend. I pushed the thoughts away. Already it was hard to imagine letting this little one go.

* * *

By the time we got home the next afternoon, the pain-softening effect of the anaesthetic had completely worn off and Megan was in a lot of discomfort. Irritated by the arm restraints she was wearing to prevent her from pulling at her wound and still sore and swollen from the operation, she continued to shun her bottle. She cried at the mere sight of it, shaking her head furiously from side to side when she saw the teat coming towards her.

For some reason, the little rascal had no objection to her dummy, sucking on it as if her life depended on it. Thankfully she enjoyed taking milk from a spoon. It was a time-consuming way to feed her, but she was able to keep more of it down that way. After every feed I filled a syringe with cooled boiled water and rinsed her mouth to help prevent infection, something else she wasn't at all impressed with.

For an hour or so after each dose of Calpol she brightened enough to sit on the floor, propped up with several cushions, her toys set out in front of her. Though she was only just over three months old she could already sit for a few seconds unaided before flopping back and smiled proudly when we applauded her efforts. For the rest of the day she kept me on my feet, wailing if I dared to sit down for even a minute.

As the days passed the stitches dissolved and the swelling went down. A week later there was barely any sign of the cleft at all. It was hard to visualise how she had looked before the repair and I marvelled at the surgeon's skill. Whenever she caught sight of one of us she beamed, but we had all grown so used to the gap in her lip that it was strange to see her without it. Part of me missed the old, lopsided smile.

Chapter Fifteen

'She's bi-polar,' Peggy boomed over a crackle of static. It was mid-February 2012, four months after Megan's operation and I was pushing a double pram along the icy riverside path towards the park. On one side sat Megan, her mittened hands cupped over the front bar, her favourite blanket clutched in between. Zadie's baby, Nailah, was sleeping beneath several blankets on the other side, tiny breaths wispy in the air above her face.

Born on a cold night in November, Nailah's arrival saw another change in our lives, one that I was still trying to adjust to – Des left for the US a few days after Zadie brought her baby daughter home. Positive and worldly wise, it had always been a comfort to know that he was only ever a phone call away and, though I suspected that he was one of those gregarious people indiscriminate with their affection, my fondness for him had grown, more than I had ever intended. When he came to say goodbye, unexpectedly one evening, he invited us to go to America with him. I was so surprised, and so touched, that I barely even responded. As the days passed and I heard nothing from him, I felt bad about that. Whenever he crept into mind, I felt a nagging ache in my chest, and sometimes I doubted my decision.

With Zadie back at school and two little ones to care for, the weeks had passed in a flurry of washing cycles and feeding regimes. Apart from short trips to the supermarket or brisk strolls to the library or soft play, we battened down the hatches, hardly leaving the house in the weeks leading up to Christmas.

At seven months, Megan could roll from one end of the room to the other and drag herself forward using her elbows, commando style. Occasionally she'd lift her little bottom in the air in imitation of a crawl but giggled so hard at the feat that she'd collapse and bump her nose on the carpet. She was still way below her ideal weight, although a combination of solid food and her ability to sit for longer periods had eased the worst of her reflux. After weeks of trying, I finally gave up offering her milk in a bottle, resorting to a soft spouted cup instead.

Teething seemed to put her off the dummy as well, so I stopped offering that at the same time, and was surprised to find that she barely seemed to notice its absence. Instead I rubbed some Ashton & Parson's teething powders gently into her gums before bed – the effect was stunning, and she slept for six hours straight. Every mother in the area seemed to discover its magical properties at the same time, though, and for a few weeks it was impossible to get hold of. The elusive packages mysteriously appeared on eBay for treble the usual price, but I couldn't bring myself to buy any through fear that they might be fake goods filled with talcum powder, or something far worse.

Megan's nose and lip healed well, the redness of the scar fading to a pale pink that was almost invisible unless you really looked for it. We quickly grew accustomed to the new look, although she had been just as beautiful before.

Nailah, even though she was months younger, weighed only a few pounds less than Megan so that, side by side, there was barely any difference between the two of them in size. The similarities ended there though. Where Nailah's skin was honey-toned, Megan's was paper white. Nailah seemed more robust than Megan as well, solid and strong-limbed. Megan always seemed to be slightly under the weather, regular ear infections and courses of antibiotics lowering her resistance to the coughs and colds doing the rounds at mother and toddler group. Nailah, on the other hand, never caught even the most fleeting of sniffles. By nature they were chalk and cheese as well. Megan was fearless and prone to dangerous pursuits – at home she scrambled onto the sofa and threw herself off without the slightest hesitation, even before she had mastered a proper crawl, whereas Nailah's movements were precise and gentle, quietly reserved like her mum.

From the minute they woke me in the morning until the blessed moment I fell into bed late in the evening, I was busy. Between preparing meals and feeding them, changing nappies, washing their clothes and playing, there was barely a moment to spare, but I enjoyed being so absorbed that there wasn't time to think about anything else. There were times when I felt lonely, those occasional days most mothers experience at some point or another, when the hollow spot inside me refused to be ignored. Not that I was complaining – they were beautiful babies and I loved the endless entertainment of watching them interact.

Using one hip as leverage, I eased the buggy around to give Megan a better view of the river and pulled down the rain cover on Nailah's side to protect her from the cold air. The plastic flapped in noisy protest, straining against its elasticised pegs. I secured the brake and crouched beside Megan, cupping my hand over my ear to stop the wind whistling through the handset. 'Who is?' I asked Peggy. 'Do you mean Christina?' She always did this, launching straight into the middle of a conversation as if greetings and details were trifling nuisances she simply didn't have time for.

'No, no,' she said, like an irritated, old-fashioned schoolmarm. 'Hayley, I'm talking about Hayley. You know, Christina's friend, the one who wanted to be assessed. By all accounts she's not very reliable with her medication, and she's got a history of self-harm. There's no way we can take her forward on that basis.'

'OK,' I said neutrally, though secretly I was relieved. I watched as the wind swept across the water, the surface corrugating in choppy little waves that mirrored the brooding, streaky grey sky. A line of ducks peaked and dipped soundlessly with the tide, stopping now and again to dip their heads beneath the surface of the water. To Megan's delight, two changed course and waddled over the mudbank towards us. She stretched over, trying to touch them. They pecked at the air near her mittens and she looked at me in awe. I laughed softly, nodding and returning her look of wonder. 'And Christina? Is she still in the picture?' When the contact supervisors brought Megan back from seeing her mum, they often stopped for a few minutes to chat. From their perspective, contact had been going well, Christina interacting positively with Megan and instinctively offering her the comfort she needed.

'She's doing brilliantly. I frogmarched her back to rehab, though we're not supposed to get involved so I wouldn't tell anyone else that, and since then she's kept them up.'

'So she'll go on to full assessment?'

'No. It's too late for her, I'm afraid. Her hair-strand test came back and confirmed that she was still using after Megan was born. She'd need to be clean for a lot longer than that before we could take a chance on her, way beyond Megan's timescales.'

'And she agrees?'

'Her consent is being dispensed with,' Peggy said, meaning, in social work terms, that Christina was likely to lose her parental rights, however much she fought against it, provided, of course, that a judge agreed with social services decision. 'She's supportive of her father's application though. Christina's mother left the marriage when

Christina was very young. Jem did his best to bring her up alone but she took to drink at 14. She doesn't blame him, says she just got in with the wrong crowd. I think it might be a workable solution that suits everyone.'

The social worker's voice sounded thick as if she were drinking. 'The initial checks on Jem and the partner are clear so there's no reason not to take them onto full assessment. I've asked them to attend a parenting workshop to show their commitment, and we'll see what happens from there.'

'How long before we know more?' I asked distractedly. Megan had begun to moan so I released her straps and lifted her one-handed, out of the pram. At the water's edge, I crouched down and hoisted her onto my knee. Pointing across the water, I signalled two swans with my eyes, emerging from beneath the overhanging willows. Circling each other with antagonistic, jerky movements, they exchanged low, wheezy whistles, their wings arched wide. Megan stared, enraptured. She kicked her legs excitedly. As they drifted closer she shrank away, hands clamouring to catch hold of me. 'It's all right,' I whispered, straightening. She huddled against me, burrowing her face into my neck.

From the other end of the line came a clink of crockery and then Peggy answered: 'How long is a piece of string?' It was a typically blunt response and there wasn't really much I could say to that. I nodded futilely and tucked Megan back into her pram. Squatting in front of her, I tugged on her woollen hat, pulling it down to nestle around her ears.

I heard a slurp, and then after a loud gulp Peggy said, 'Of course, you do realise there's nothing to stop you throwing your hat in the ring, don't you?'

I squinted, frowning. 'I don't follow.'

'Adoption,' she said, and I could picture her waving her hand impatiently as if her meaning was obvious. My free hand dropped slowly, coming to rest next to Megan's on the front bar. 'I'd happily support any application from you if you wanted to put yourself forward as an adopter for Megan.'

Water lapped at the bank, birds circling above. I listened silently, too surprised to respond. 'I thought I'd mention it,' Peggy added in the pause. 'There's plenty of time to think about it. It might not be something you'd consider, but she seems to be thriving in your care.'

One of the gulls screeched loudly overhead. I looked up and straightened, rising to my feet. Megan's face fell. She turned her head and looked up at me, frowning. 'But I wouldn't be allowed to adopt, would I?'

'Why ever not?' Peggy wheezed.

'Well, for a start I'm divorced. I don't even own my own home.'

'And?'

'And so, they'd never let me.'

'Nonsense,' Peggy barked. 'None of those things precludes you from being considered – we're not interested in social engineering, you know, whatever tales certain elements of the press like to bandy around. Of course, you're in for disappointment if her grandfather is approved, or someone else happens to be a better match for Megan, but you might feel you want to take that chance. Personally I think you'd make a wonderful adopter,' she added, her warm words at odds with her brisk tone. 'Now, I really must get on.'

She ended the call without further conversation. I lowered my mobile phone and stared at the blank screen, my mind suddenly whirling.

Chapter Sixteen

The children's play area was swathed in ribbons of feathery mist, grey clouds swelling above our heads. It really was cold, but several hardy children were playing on the ice-covered equipment, their mothers stamping their feet and rubbing their gloved hands together nearby. I parked the pram near a small scooter propped up against the black metal railings and walked around the front, reaching a hand underneath the rain cover and pulling the blankets up around Nailah's chin. Megan stretched out her short arms as soon as she saw me, a sight that never failed to melt my heart. 'Come on then, sweetheart,' I said, zipping her thick coat up as high as it would go, straightening her hat and then unclipping her straps again. I pulled her to me and planted kisses on her forehead.

She lifted her face and sucked my chin affectionately, her mouth warm on my skin. Her small hands clamped my cheeks possessively and soon she began to gnaw, her gums clamping down with surprising pressure. 'Hey, you!' I cried, laughing as I arched my face away. I lowered her into the nearest swing. She gurgled a laugh, two bright red teething spots glowing above the dimples on her cheeks.

I grabbed her blanket from the pram and rolled it up, squeezing it between her and the back of the swing to keep her steady. 'Ready? Are you steady?' She bobbed around, answering with a stream of excited babble. 'Right, up we go then. Whee!' I pushed gently on the swing and her mouth dropped in a wide smile, eyes shiny and bright. With her hearing problems I wasn't sure how much she took in, but she was making lots of sounds in response to my own, new ones each day.

'Mama-mama-ma,' she said, smiling at me lovingly.

'Not Mama, R-o-sie,' I corrected, though my heart stirred at the sound.

'Mama-mama-ma,' she said.

I smiled and turned around, my attention caught by a small boy as he charged across the sandpit behind us. He was a stocky little chap around two years old and something in the way he moved evoked memories of Harry, one of the siblings I had cared for years earlier. After years of fostering it was often that way; children floating into my mind, their faces slightly out of focus, like little ghosts. I hadn't seen Harry since he moved onto adoptive parents with his sister, but I never forgot his special ways and how fearless he was. I always had to make sure the first-aid box was well stocked when he was around. Smiling to myself, I watched as the little boy clambered to the top of the slide then raised his hands in triumph. Without warning he cheered then leapt off, landing on his bottom with a thud and, after a moment's hesitation, a whimper. His mother shouted at him in exasperation then, but picked him up and gave him a hug.

I looked back at Megan, wondering whether it might really be possible for us to keep her.

At home Megan sat in her high chair sucking on some thin slices of apple while I warmed some milk for Nailah. At the sight of the bottle Megan started to fuss, so I quickly made one up for her as well, though I knew what was likely to happen when I gave it to her. After testing it on the inside of my wrist I offered it to her, but as soon as the teat touched her tongue she pulled a lemon face and pushed it away.

I pulled up a chair and sat in front of Megan while I gave Nailah her bottle. I loved watching her eat; the intrigue crossing her features as she worked her way through the nibbles on her tray. I couldn't stop smiling as her small hand hovered over a stick of carrot like one of those robotic arms in a fairground machine full of soft toys. With Herculean effort, her fingers descended until she finally closed her fist around the prize. Turning the sliver first one way and then the other, she examined it with exceptional diligence and then stuck it in one of her ears.

I loved the idea of baby-led weaning and had read all about it online, but very little finger food actually seemed to make it into Megan's mouth, so I could never resist offering her some mushy food as well. After settling Nailah in her bouncy chair I heated some pureed salmon and sweet potato that I'd cooked in a large batch and separated into ice cubes, and put the dish in front of Megan. I gave her a spoon of her own to hold and then offered her a tiny taste of the unfamiliar meal.

She opened her mouth wide and then stared at me with a look of surprise, her cheeks moving rhythmically as she chewed. Unsure at first, she took the first few spoonfuls with a wary eye on me. 'Yum, yum,' I said, nodding and pretending to try and nibble some myself.

Grinning, she slapped a flat hand in the food, closing her fist around it. Eagerly, she sucked on her hand, the orange gloop running over her wrists and disappearing up her sleeves.

I laughed, dabbing the dribble from her small round chin. 'You're a funny little pickle, yes you are.'

Already I looked upon her as my own child, but the idea of keeping her hadn't even crossed my mind until Peggy mentioned it. I wanted her to stay with us; there was no doubt about that, but I knew it wasn't really about what I wanted. What mattered was Megan and, ultimately, what was best for her. And of course, there was Emily and Jamie to think about. They had always enjoyed fostering and, although there had been some difficult times, they had drawn lots of positives from it.

But accepting a child permanently into their family, as their own sister, was something else entirely. I had a feeling they might jump at the chance but it was a big assumption to make and anyway, with Christina's father still keen to adopt Megan, there wasn't much point in discussing it with them until we knew more.

Chapter Seventeen

The nights shortened and the skies grew lighter, the passing months bringing more changes to our family. Some were thrilling, Megan perfecting the art of crawling and following us around the house at lightning speed, Emily completing her GCSEs, Jamie managing to play the whole first verse of 'Moon River' on the guitar without losing patience and snatching up his Xbox controls instead.

But the most shocking event was undoubtedly Zadie going missing. When I first registered with Bright Heights Fostering Agency, my assessing social worker told me that foster carers had to be prepared for anything, and in April, when Zadie didn't return home from school, her words flew back to me with a vengeance.

Though the little ones were largely unaware of what was going on, Nailah was disorientated by the loss of her mum and I think both she and Megan sensed there was something wrong. Usually smiley and good-natured, their moods changed and they cried easily, staring at me with perplexed, worried frowns. It was a tumultuous time but ended, thankfully, with Zadie's return a week after she went missing. The family members involved in taking her were arrested and, to our delight, Zadie and her elder sister were reunited with their mother soon afterwards. The teenager left us in July, taking Nailah to start a new life with her birth family.

Megan was almost a year old by then and for a few days afterwards she crawled from room to room with a bleak expression, searching for her missing playmate. I offered her lots of cuddles and tried to explain, but the idea that their lives were continuing away from ours was complicated, way beyond her comprehension.

We spent the quiet days following their departure in the garden, playing with sand and water, arranging Megan's soft toys in a circle and cutting sandwiches into tiny triangles for a teddy bears' picnic. I missed Zadie and Nailah, but it was lovely to spend some time alone with Megan.

The whirlwind arrival of Mack, a 14-year-old boy who came to stay as an emergency placement after a fall-out with his stepfather, briefly interrupted the tranquillity, but Megan, at that magical stage on the cusp of taking her first steps, quickly worked her charms on him. She pottered between us with big, dribbling smiles and Mack's sullen scowl melted instantly whenever she rested her hand on his tracksuit-covered knee. When he left three days later, my heart melted as he swept her up into the air and allowed her to plant wet kisses on his cheek.

Another change to our routine came when Peggy suspended contact after Christina's repeated non-attendance. All birth parents were regularly warned that the local authority operated a strict 'three strikes and you're out' policy, and most were careful to avoid missing any more than two in a row. Since contact had switched to the family centre I had kept a diary, packing it in the bag that went with Megan to contact alongside her milk, nappies and spare clothes. Inside I wrote regular updates on Megan: her latest weight, vaccinations, any new sounds she made, and Christina's enthusiastic replies showed her interest. Her sudden absence puzzled me. When I spoke to Peggy about it, she shared her suspicion that Christina had relapsed into drug dependency again. On the bright side, there was less running around and, apart from the weekly contact with Jem, her grandfather, which seemed to be going well, our days were our own.

Without the daily reminder of contact, it was easy to forget that I was fostering Megan and with each passing day it became more and more impossible to imagine our lives without her. Once Peggy had planted the idea of adoption in my mind it was difficult to nudge it away and I longed to talk to Emily and Jamie about the possibility of keeping Megan, but I didn't want to mention anything, particularly as her grandfather's assessment seemed to be progressing well.

It was late July and Megan was just over 12 months old when the chance finally arrived. The two of us were in the garden, Megan crouching on her haunches beside me as I pulled up weeds, her little dress ruffling up at the hem. With her own small garden fork in one hand and matching shovel in the other, she dug over the soft earth, fountains of soil spraying the air. Every so often she downed tools and half-staggered, half-crawled over to pick up a plant spray, industriously covering our tomato plants with a fine mist of water. She babbled away as she worked, her faltering words barely comprehensible but adorable all the same. My heart soared whenever I heard a word I vaguely recognised. 'Dig, dig,' she said, looking up at me with a proud smile.

'Yes, you're digging, clever girl!'

Across the garden, a robin appeared. Megan stilled, captivated by the bird as it fluttered its wings and came to rest on the top of our low stone wall. It skittered along the top, halting every few steps to survey its surroundings. She pointed, one of her latest tricks. Half a second later she was off, her feet carrying her faster than her body was able to go. Losing her footing, she tumbled over, arms flying out in front of her for balance, nappy-covered bottom sticking out from beneath her rumpled dress. 'Oops-a-daisy,' I called out, and after a short pause she was on her feet again, smiling.

We pottered for hours, the sounds of summer – an occasional splosh of water from the leaky outside pipe, the companionable chatter of our elderly neighbours, low and soft, from the garden next door, the chink of metal against china as they stirred their tea – conspiring to muddle our sense of time. I only realised we hadn't eaten lunch when the telephone rang. 'My goodness, Meggie, it's nearly half past one,' I said, patting the soil from my hands and racing to pick up my handset.

'There's been a bust-up,' Peggy said as soon as I pressed the SEND button.

'A-ha,' I answered and then waited for the social worker to continue. With Peggy, I had learned to let the conversation flow at her own pace. Asking questions had a tendency to slow up proceedings and make her bad-tempered.

'The police were called. Jem's in custody but he's made a counter-allegation against the partner. It's all a big mess. No, not that one,' she added impatiently, her voice suddenly muffled. 'The white printer, over there. Sorry, Rosie, I wasn't talking to you.' There was a tapping sound, an impatient tutting. 'Where was I?'

Peggy continued with the tale, pausing intermittently to answer a colleague or take a gulp of tea. From what I could make out, there had been a domestic between Christina's father, Jem, and his partner, Jackie. I sat in my wicker chair and listened, the sun warming my face, Megan doddering busily to and fro. I could hear her twittering to herself. Every so often she stopped, pointing to something of interest. 'In a nutshell, things aren't looking too hopeful for them. Well, what I mean is, they've effectively ruled themselves out. There's no way I can take them forward, even if neither of them are charged. So, if you want to be considered, Rosie, now's the time to put your intentions in writing.'

My heart soared with happiness as Peggy ended the call. I sat for a moment, embracing the phone to my chest.

Across the garden, Megan had stopped mid-crawl beside a large shrub. Grasping the leaves, she ran her thumb over the dark glossy folds, small mouth pursed in concentration, cheeks rosy from the sun. Rising on bent knees, she leaned in closer, staring fixedly.

'What is it, sweetie?' I asked, moving to kneel at her side. 'Oh, I see,' I whispered. About three inches from her nose, a bee was hovering above a velvety white flower. 'That's a bumble bee,' I said. She turned to me, her eyes suddenly snapping shut in a sneeze. She blinked and shook her head, eyes wide with wonder and then her head wobbled as another sneeze took hold. 'Ah, bless you,' I laughed, tapping my forefinger on her nose. She giggled and threw her short arms around my neck. My heart swelled at the thought that she might one day be ours.

I couldn't wait for Emily and Jamie to get home so that I could discuss the possibility with them.

Chapter Eighteen

Having spent months imagining how they might react, I felt a tightening in my chest as I waited for Emily and Jamie to come home. If they showed the slightest reluctance to the idea of keeping Megan, I knew I couldn't possibly even consider the idea again. I also knew they'd be tired – my ex-husband, Gary, and his new partner, Tammy, had managed to get tickets to watch the basketball down at the Olympic Park in London and they'd left before 5 a.m. that morning – but I didn't want to put off the conversation any longer. With Megan tucked up in bed, I busied myself in the kitchen, wiping surfaces that were already clean and drinking far too much tea.

They got back at twilight; the sun softening as it lowered itself over the garden. At the sound of Gary's car I kneeled up on the sofa to peer outside. Gary climbed out of the driver's side, gave Emily a hug and ruffled Jamie's hair. Tammy, red-haired and pretty, stayed where she was but lowered her window and called something out as they crossed the drive. I couldn't hear what she said but the pair of them turned in unison and burst out laughing, Emily stopping to give them a friendly wave as they drove away. I felt a tiny pang in my chest at the sight.

'How was it?' I asked, meeting them in the hall. I forced a jolly tone, trying hard to suppress the niggle of envy in my stomach, the childish part of me feeling left out of what had clearly been an enjoyable family trip. It felt odd to know that, even though I had acknowledged years earlier that there would be no chance of reconciliation, there was now no way back to the nuclear family I had always hoped to be part of. I had often worried about the effect our divorce might have on the children in years to come and I felt a stab of resentment towards Gary for putting them through the awkwardness of meeting another new partner. At the same time I knew it wasn't reasonable to feel that way. He had a right to make a life for himself.

'It was so cool!' Jamie cried, tossing himself onto the sofa. 'We watched some diving as well as the basketball. And we went to the velodrome as well. There wasn't any cycling going on, but Dad got talking to one of the trainers on Team GB and he showed us some of the bikes. They're amazing!'

I summoned an even bigger smile. 'Fabulous! Ems, did you enjoy yourself?'

She eyed me cautiously. 'It's a beautiful place, Mum. The only downside was all the sport.' Jamie rolled his eyes at that. She jutted her chin, threw him a look. 'But I loved the park, and lunch was nice.'

'What did you have?'

'Oh, nothing special really,' Emily said, averting her gaze. She was being kind, bless her, but my heart twisted; I didn't want her to feel it was her job to protect my feelings. I reminded myself of the time I was asked by a birth parent to stop taking her child swimming, ''cos she'll expect to do that sort of thing all the time when she gets back home and I don't want her spoilt'. Going to the Olympics was a once-in-a-lifetime experience and I knew I should have been pleased that they'd been able to go.

Jamie raised his head. 'What? Yeah, it was. Tammy's got this huge picnic basket with proper glasses and knives and forks and stuff. She brought chicken wings and pork ribs and wraps and so much salad.' He bunched his fingers together, kissing the tips noisily as he smacked his lips. 'It was like being at Nando's.'

I felt really bugged then. 'How about that?!' I said, raising my eyes minutely in Emily's direction. Jamie carried on raving about his day, but Emily met my gaze and put the back of her hand to her mouth, stifling giggles. Somehow, that tiny acknowledgement of my feelings made them seem misplaced and ridiculously overblown. I laughed back. My heart felt lighter.

A bit later, after they'd showered, I sat between them on the sofa and readied myself to broach the subject of Megan. 'I've been thinking,' I said tentatively, resting my head back on a cushion and running the tips of my fingers over the inside of my palm in an effort to look casual. 'What would you think about Megan staying here permanently?'

Emily, who had been curled up against the armrest, swung her legs to the floor and sat up. She looked at me, brow furrowed. 'Permanently? How could she?'

I lifted my head. 'Well, we could ask to adopt her, if you both think it's a good idea.'

'Oh, my God, really?' She clasped her hands. 'Can we? Really?'

I nodded, smiling. 'Peggy seems to think so.'

'Oh, wow! I've always wanted a sister!' She looked across at Jamie, who, less excitable than his sister, took longer to react.

'Well, Jamie?' I prompted, although I could already tell by the curl of his lips that he liked the idea. 'What do you think?'

He shrugged. 'I'm already outnumbered. What difference will one more girl make?'

Emily clasped my hands. We stared at each other for a moment, then leapt from the sofa and jumped around the room like excited five-year-olds.

Chapter Nineteen

The next day, when Emily was in her room, I sat beside Jamie on the sofa and asked him to pause the online football game he was playing so that we could have a chat. 'What's up?' he asked, one eyebrow half-cocked.

'Did you mean what you said about Megan? You're not just saying it because you think it's what I want to hear?'

When it was just the two of us he often dropped the cool teenage persona and morphed into someone younger. He leaned into me, bestowing the most affectionate hug he was able to give while clutching his gaming handset. 'Course not. I love Megan,' he said simply. 'I've always wanted more brothers and sisters.'

'You're sure? You wouldn't just say that?'

'Nah,' he answered, but he already sounded vague. I studied him for a few seconds, the new angles to his chin, the leanness of his cheeks. Time passed so quickly.

'Because if you're trying to please me …' I started up again. His eyes drifted from me to the TV screen and slowly, reluctantly, back again. 'Or Emily, or you think it might sound mean to say you'd rather not keep her –'

'Mum,' he cut in, resting the handset on his lap with a long-suffering sigh. 'I'm not being rude, but can you stop talking now? Cos I didn't get to play *FIFA* at all yesterday and every second we deliberate over this is another second I lag behind Ben. And if that happens my game plan is wrecked.' He raised his eyebrows. 'D'you really want that on your conscience?'

Thrilled by their reaction, I called my mum later that day to see what she thought. 'But you're on your own,' she said, sounding a little scandalised, although I sensed a frisson of excitement there too.

Soon after I separated from Gary I dug up the small garden in our first rented house with the intention of installing a lobster farm to make ends meet. Standing in a boggy mess after three days of digging, my fingers dotted with blisters, I found my enthusiasm waning. Ever since then Mum seemed to hold the view that I was wild and flighty. She still had kittens whenever I told her of one of my plans and seemed to feel the need to rein me in, playing devil's advocate to make sure I'd thought through all the many ways good ideas can turn sour.

'That doesn't matter apparently.'

There was a pause. 'No, I suppose it doesn't. There's nothing to stop anyone doing anything nowadays,' she said, with a trace of disappointment. 'If they're going to let transvestites and what have you adopt I don't see why you shouldn't be allowed. They *do*, you know,' she stated insistently, as if I'd argued the point. 'I saw it on a recruitment poster on the back of a bus the other day.' A traditionalist and loyal reader of the *Daily Mail*, Mum was still struggling to come to terms with the installation of self-service checkouts in supermarkets. And the arrival of a gay couple in the maisonette above hers very nearly blew her mind. 'They're civilly partnershipped, you know,' she told her every visitor with a sort of confused pride, as if she were the first person in England to be able to make such a claim.

'Not that I'm against it,' she said now. 'Your grandmother would turn in her grave, but I'm not one to judge, you know me.'

I couldn't suppress a snort at that.

'What?' she demanded, sounding injured. 'Each to their own. What people do in the privacy of their own home isn't any of my business. I just think it must a bit confusing, that's all. Coming home from school and finding Daddy on the sofa, wearing a dress. Imagine!' She gave a little titter. 'You wouldn't know whether you were coming or going, you really wouldn't.'

'So, anyway, Mum, what do you think about Megan?'

'Oh goodness, someone else to worry about? Another mouth to feed? I love the little dot to pieces but haven't you got enough on your plate?'

And so it was decided. I sent Peggy an email that evening and told her that I'd love to be considered to adopt Megan. She responded enthusiastically, saying that she was thrilled for all of us. I knew several foster carers who had been flatly refused when they asked to be considered as adopters for the children they were looking after, so I was heartened by her reaction. A few months earlier a fostering friend of mine, Jenny, made an application to keep Billy, a four-year-old boy who had lived with her for over a year. The local authority, fearing that Jenny might abscond with the child, had hurriedly arranged another placement for him.

'Don't tell me, I know,' Mum said with mock exasperation when I called her the next morning. 'Honest to goodness, I can't keep up with it all,' she added, but I could tell she was pleased.

The possibility of keeping Megan began to seem all the more real.

Chapter Twenty

The following month, at the beginning of September, Peggy surprised us with an unexpected visit. 'I won't stay long,' she said without preliminaries, heavy rain beating down on the path behind her. Megan had followed me along the hall with the sweet little hum she always made when she crawled around – it was like being stalked by a large bumble bee – and clasped a fist around the leg of my jeans. With a loud oomph, she hauled herself to her feet and peered up at Peggy with a beaming smile.

'Hello, trouble,' the social worker said, looking down at her. She sounded reserved, no trace of her usual gusto.

'Come here, pickle,' I said, hoiking Megan onto my hip. Peggy turned and came into the house backwards, shaking her umbrella over the front step and then collapsing it down. I was beginning to feel uneasy. Peggy's expression was grave as she tipped forward with a groan and rested the brolly against the wall. She looked close to tears. I squeezed her arm. 'Are you all right? Have you brought bad news about Megan?' Instinctively I held the toddler a little closer.

'Oh no, nothing like that. We're waiting for DNA results on someone who came forward claiming to be the father, but there's been nothing back as yet. No,' she said heavily, as she followed me through to the kitchen. She moved slowly, devoid of her usual industrious bounce. 'There has been a complaint. I've been suspended while it's being investigated.'

'Oh no, Peggy! I'm sorry,' I said, feeling guiltily relieved that it was nothing to do with our application to adopt. I lowered Megan to the floor and pulled out a stool for Peggy. She sank down on it with a gasp, the damp hem of her skirt clinging to her brown nylon tights. 'What happened, or would you rather not say?'

'Oh, I don't mind saying all right. These bloody liberals, they make my blood boil. Would you mind?' she said suddenly, banging her chest and inclining her head towards the kettle. 'I'm parched.'

I shook my head. 'Oh yes, sorry.' As I reached across the worktop, Megan began to complain. Peggy reached down and pulled her onto her lap with another loud groan. Megan didn't object but her eyes widened at the sudden change of perspective. She looked at me, questioning. I smiled and she relaxed, snuggling back into the social worker's ample chest. A few minutes later I handed Peggy a mug of steaming tea and Megan some milk. 'Is that strong enough?'

'It's wet and warm, that'll do me,' Peggy wheezed, seizing the mug and trying to fend off Megan's inquisitive hand, which was straying down the front of her blouse. I reached for the toddler and sat her on the worktop in front of me, looping her short legs around my trunk so that she wouldn't fall off. Megan watched Peggy gulping down her tea with interest. 'It all came about after I spoke to Christina about getting fitted with a long-term contraceptive device,' confided Peggy, 'on account of the fact that if she doesn't, she's likely to be pregnant again before the ink is dry on Megan's adoption certificate. She will, you know, left to her own devices. So anyway, I suggested, gently mind,' she lifted one of her hands in mock surrender and I bit down on my lip to suppress a smile; it was difficult to imagine Peggy doing anything subtly, 'that she consider it an option.'

I grimaced. 'And she didn't take it well?'

Peggy leaned back and let out a huff of exasperation. 'Well, that's just the thing. *She* didn't take offence at all. She seemed to think it wasn't a bad idea. Having Megan really took it out of her, physically and emotionally. I think she desperately wants a way out of the destructive cycle she's in. She's just not strong enough to do it alone.'

I frowned. 'But she complained anyway?'

'No, *she* didn't. That's what I'm trying to tell you. One of my colleagues overheard the conversation and couldn't resist putting her two-penneth in, but not to me directly. She reported me to the management. Now I've been suspended for inappropriate behaviour. Apparently my advice went against Christina's rights as a woman. They said I'm trying to, and I quote, "impose my own set of values onto someone else". She nodded at me fervently, her jaw lowered, as if she couldn't quite believe what she was saying. 'I'm guilty of making moral judgements apparently. So I said, "What about little Megan's rights? She's going to be a woman one day. And because of Christina's habit she may very well have hearing or learning difficulties or goodness knows what else. Don't we have a duty of care towards her as well? You go on about rights, but what about Megan's rights?" They couldn't come up for an answer for that now, could they?' She shook her head. 'The Americans pay addicts to get sterilised, did you know that?' I opened my mouth but she spoke again before I could say anything. 'They seem to have the right idea over there. Where is good old British common sense these days?' She sighed. 'I'm used to hearing hogwash in my line of work, I can tell you, but this really takes the biscuit.'

I shook my head in sympathy. My initial reservations about Peggy – her expression of disapproval that I came to realise had more to do with a wayward chin than any real sentiment, her tendency to blurt out whatever she thought without running it through a filter first – had evaporated quickly. Forthright, guileless and warm, she didn't care a jot for convention, but she was so dedicated to her job and, above all, she genuinely cared. I could imagine that her attempts to guide Christina in from the shadowy edges of society may have been a bit clumsy, but it was difficult to believe that anyone could doubt that her heart was in the right place.

Megan sucked loudly on her milk. When the cup was nearly empty she tipped it sideways, banging it on my head. 'Oi!' I said, whipping it away. She giggled as I put her down, then pulled herself up using the leg of one of the stools. She skirted Peggy's legs and began playing with the laces of her flat shoes. Peggy smiled down at her absent-mindedly and then looked back at me, her watery eyes looking suddenly wearisome. 'If truth be told this was a long time coming. I've felt something brewing for a while now. I've been told I'm unsociable, and apparently I make people feel uncomfortable.'

'Oh, Peggy, that's rubbish! I feel like I've known you for years. Some people don't like hearing the truth,' I added, realising how much I sounded like my mother.

Peggy threw me a grateful smile, her heavy chin wobbling. 'Even my own colleagues snubbed me when I cleared my desk. They're all terrified of getting tarred with the same brush, I suppose.' She made an attempt to laugh, but her lip quivered. We both turned sharply to noise in the hall, and then Jamie appeared. 'Ah,' Peggy said, sounding suddenly, miraculously, cheerful, 'here's your young man. Well, I've leave you to get on, Rosie.'

'Bam-Bam!' Megan shrieked, letting go of the stool and hovering, trying to get her balance. She managed six or seven steps and then stumbled over, dropping to her hands and knees. Jamie grinned at the sight of her. He crouched down, picked up one of her toys and jangled it. She shuffled towards him, talking gobbledegook, her little bottom wriggling as she attempted a speedy crawl.

The social worker faltered as she walked down the hall. I put out my hand to steady her. 'Will you be OK, Peggy?'

She blinked over the damp film on her eyes. 'Oh, I'll be fine. Doesn't do to dwell on things, does it? I might take myself off somewhere nice while all this is going on. I've always fancied the Isle of Man. Except,' she paused, producing a handkerchief from her sleeve and pressing it to her mouth, 'I don't quite know what to do with myself when I'm not working.'

I pulled a sympathetic face and rubbed her chunky shoulder. I got the impression that she lived for her work, and punishing her for trying to make a difference seemed to me to be a travesty. The sad thing was, as far as I knew, there was no husband or children in her life to share the upset with. She spoke of her animals with great fondness though, so at least she might find some comfort there. I stood at the door, my heart going out to her as she trundled down the path through the downpour. Shimmering curtains of rain rolled down the sides of her umbrella, heavy drops bouncing up from the path to drench her stout calves, her flat grey shoes.

Looking back, part of me still wonders whether what happened with Megan might have been avoided, if only Peggy had still been responsible for her care.

Chapter Twenty-One

The months passed, notching up new achievements, newly learned skills to delight in. In early October there were about five recognisable words in Megan's vocabulary, and by the end of the month she had mastered 15. She was using them to good effect as well, mostly trying to guide us towards her way of thinking. 'No, Mama!' was an oft-used phrase, spoken with such a bossy tone that we couldn't help but laugh.

It was fascinating to watch her little personality emerging, each day producing new facets, and never-before-seen facial expressions to accompany them. In some of her gestures I saw flashes of my own, or Emily's or Jamie's, the recognition always catching me by surprise.

If things didn't go her way she was prone to the most ferocious temper tantrums, the sight of which was so alarming that bystanders sometimes felt the need to stop and offer emergency assistance.

The most violent of her meltdowns were usually triggered by visitors (often social workers) who drew my attention away from her. At the suggestion of a fostering friend of mine, I bought Megan an egg timer. Whenever she grew tetchy, I set the timer and told her that when the buzzer went off I would play with her. It worked well on occasion, but tended to bring any conversation I was having to an abrupt end.

Towards the end of October, the day before Halloween, my childless friend Helen popped over, unannounced, on one of her rare afternoons off. 'I'm toying with the idea of giving up completely,' she mumbled between mouthfuls of homemade lemon cake, in the throes of giving me the low-down on her latest dalliances in the online dating world. 'It's exhausting and demoralising. I don't know why I bother. All I really need is a glass of wine in one hand and a slab of cake in the other.'

Offended by the loss of my undivided attention, Megan grew increasingly disgruntled. Half an hour into the visit she began bashing the receiver of her toy telephone against her own head. I was about to distract her when Helen said 'No' in a gently chiding voice, pointing out that her discomfort was a direct result of her own silliness.

Megan was fond of the word 'No', but not so keen when it was used against her. She looked up at Helen with a non-committal expression, tinkering with the idea of letting things slide. It could have gone either way at that point, but then Helen raised her eyebrows in a warning fashion. Megan gave a small half-hearted scream then stopped to reassess our reaction. There was still everything to play for but the horrified expression on Helen's face settled the matter. Megan exploded, roaring until the skin on her face bordered on purple. 'What in the name of sanity is going on?!' Helen cried, the colour fading from her own cheeks. 'Rosie, do something!'

'Don't be daft,' I said calmly, sliding off the sofa. Once Megan reached full throttle, nothing short of a firework display could distract her, although the smoke alarm going off had once worked a treat. I knelt on the floor beside her, ready to intervene if she decided to bang her head against the floor, something she was prone to do. 'She's feeling cross, that's all. Aren't you, love? She'll be OK in a minute,' I added, throwing in a subliminal suggestion to calm her down.

'Extraordinary,' Helen declared, her eyes riveted on the convulsing child. Soon afterwards, when she'd polished off the last of the lemon cake and Megan was curled up on my lap, sobbing, Helen got up. 'I'm going home,' she announced. 'It's far too stressful here.'

Around Christmas time Megan began fixating on things. The pictures in the Alfie books by Shirley Hughes really captured her imagination and she became obsessed with one story in particular – *Dogger*, about a cuddly toy dog that goes missing. For Christmas we bought her a soft toy almost identical to the drawing in the book and, alongside the boxes of all her other new toys, it proved to be a big hit. She took Dogger to bed every night along with her beloved pink blanket and dragged it along by its ear during the day.

Her other great passion was the film *A Bug's Life*. One of her most favourite games was to act out the circus scene, although when I pretended to be the evil grasshopper, to which she was simultaneously drawn and repulsed by, she fled from the room, watching me leap around through the slightly splayed fingers covering her face. From the hallway all I could hear was terrified little squeaks, and then when I finished she would reappear, exclaiming, 'Again, again!'

By January 2013 there was still no word from social services about a replacement social worker for Megan and no news on the DNA tests in the search for her biological father. About six weeks after Peggy's temporary suspension, a locum social worker paid us a visit to run through the mandatory notification's form – a checklist designed to ascertain whether there had been any significant changes in the foster home during the course of the month, such as visits to Accident and Emergency, incidents of absconding, criminal convictions, illnesses, complaints or allegations – but she knew nothing of Megan's case and couldn't offer me any further updates.

With Christina's contact sessions still suspended and no word from anyone else, it was easy to forget that I was fostering Megan. Sometimes I felt uneasy about the unexplained delay in resolving her case, but I told myself that Peggy's colleagues were probably struggling to cope with the added burden of her cases on top of their own. It made sense for them to prioritise the ones that couldn't be left to drift.

The team at Bright Heights Fostering Agency told me that I should take the local authority's silence as a sign of trust. 'Believe me,' Lesley Evans, the manager of the agency said, when she rang to apologise for the delay in allocating a new supervising social worker to replace Des, 'if there were any concerns at all about your care they'd be all over you like a rash.'

We finally met Megan's new social worker, Hazel Cassidy, for the first time in person at the beginning of February 2013, two days after Megan's final cleft repair. She arrived at 5 p.m., one of the most dreaded times of the day for visits from officials, a cocktail of hunger and tiredness rendering children tetchy and foster carers harried. 'Come through,' I said to Hazel, hurrying back into the dining room where Megan was straining against the straps of her high chair. Hungry, but still sore from her latest operation, she began pulverising the little sandwiches I had cut into neat triangles with her fist, grinding them into her soup with an accompanying whiny squeal. 'Do you mind if we chat in here? Megan was very hungry so I couldn't keep her waiting until after our meeting.'

'Course not,' Hazel said brightly, leaning close to the high chair. 'Hello, Megan. I'm Hazel. Cor, look at all that food! That looks scrummy!'

Megan lifted her hand up to reveal a roux of squished bread, ham and tomato soup. 'Yukky-yuk,' the toddler said proudly.

'Wow, I absolutely love soup! Can't recommend it highly enough. Stuff it in your cakehole, quick!'

Megan grinned, her eyes fixed on Hazel as she sucked at the mush on her fist. The social worker laughed and sat on one of the dining chairs. Around 50 or so, she was dressed casually in a colourful jumper and black denim jeans, her chunky highlighted hair scooped up in a loose bun. A lanyard decorated with colourful badges hung from her neck, tangled up with a long silver necklace. When Megan pointed at it the social worked lifted the identity badge hanging at the end and jangled it. 'You like my pins, do you? This one's my favourite.' She pointed to one with Mickey Mouse on it and let Megan run her sticky fingers all over it. 'Do you like Mickey Mouse?'

Megan nodded. 'Mine,' she declared, clamping her hands around it.

'Ha, I don't think so, missy!' Hazel swung around theatrically and hid the badge in her armpit. Megan convulsed with laughter. When she recovered, Hazel reached into her bag. 'I've got something here you might like though,' she said, pulling out some crayons and a small notepad. 'That all right?' She looked up at me.

'Absolutely. Shall I make some drinks while you two get acquainted?' Peggy was a hard act to follow, and Hazel couldn't have been more different, but I was instantly confident that she was going to make a wonderful replacement. As much as I liked Peggy, she had never seemed all that comfortable around young children. Hazel was a natural.

'Coffee would be fabulous,' she said, flashing me a smile. She turned back to Megan, rested her elbow on the table and cradled her forehead in her hand. 'You wouldn't believe the day I've had, young lady. Oh no you wouldn't.'

Megan smiled radiantly and shook the crayons over the tray of her high chair. Hazel chatted congenially as Megan scribbled in the notebook, not in the forced way some people do with young children. In the kitchen I could hear the rise and fall of playful conversation and when I returned, Megan was sitting on Hazel's knee, chomping happily on a banana. The social worker was wearing a bit of make-up but she didn't seem to mind Megan's soupy fingers straying to her face. 'We're just getting to know one another. I hope you don't mind me getting her out? She didn't seem interested in any more of her grub. The banana's going down a treat though.'

'No, of course I don't mind. At least she's eating something,' I said, pleased that at least Megan had some fruit inside her. She'd managed some scrambled egg at lunchtime, but not much else since. She seemed quite happy on Hazel's lap. 'Do you mind?' I asked, already pulling the lid from a small pot of yoghurt.

'Go ahead,' Hazel said, 'it's like tea at Claridge's here, isn't it?' I gave Megan a teaspoon and she scooped some yoghurt from the pot, staring at it cross-eyed when it reached her mouth. Hazel made 'yum yum' noises to encourage her.

We spoke for a while about Megan's hospital stay and latest hearing test, which had shown signs of improvement. Hazel asked lots of questions, although she already seemed to have a good understanding of Megan's case. It was clear she had read the case notes thoroughly. 'I've met up with Christina and we've talked through a new contact schedule –' Hazel said, just as Megan opened her mouth in a loud yawn.

'Mama!' she cried out suddenly and threw herself towards me. I caught her under her arms and pulled her onto my lap.

'Ro-sie,' I said, correcting Megan pointedly. Foster carers who allowed looked-after children to call them affectionate family names were frowned upon, although most social workers realised that it was difficult to avoid, especially when caring for very young children. I always tried to remember to correct Megan, but I had to admit, once Peggy had suggested it might be possible to keep her, there had been times when I'd let it slip. Hazel looked unconcerned. She pulled another funny face at Megan, stuck her tongue out and blew a raspberry. I manoeuvred Megan's legs across mine so that her ear lay against my chest. She stopped moaning and snuggled into me. 'Oh, so contact is back on again? How is Christina?'

Hazel sipped her coffee then balanced her mug on Megan's tray, between bits of broken crayon and screwed-up paper. 'She's back on a programme and doing fine. I've explained the impact of no-shows on young children and she understands.'

I nodded and kissed the top of Megan's head. On the brink of sleep, she had fallen limp in my arms, her eyes open but glassy. 'Has there been any discussion about getting my assessment under way? I haven't heard anything from the adoption team.'

Hazel frowned. 'Haven't you?' She took another sip of coffee. 'Still, that might be a bit premature anyway. We haven't assessed Greg yet.'

I looked up sharply. 'Greg?'

Hazel paused. 'Yes, you know? Megan's father. Have you not been told?'

I shook my head slowly. Hazel let out a breath of annoyance. 'This is what happens when different people work the case. They came up with a DNA match a few weeks ago, just before I took over. He's working abroad at the moment, in Italy. We're waiting for the funds to be authorised so that a couple of us can go and assess him. I bet I don't get to go though.' She leaned close to Megan and pulled a pouty, sad face. Megan laughed. Hazel straightened and looked at me. 'He's thrilled at the news, although obviously very surprised. And he'd really like to get to know Megan.' Hazel tilted her head and pouted her lips when she spoke Megan's name. 'And who can blame him? You're such a gorgeous little girl, aren't you?'

I stared at her for a moment, letting the news sink in. 'I didn't know that,' I said with an inward twist. Foster carers were often the last to hear about progress in a child's case.

'I'm sorry, Rosie,' Hazel said, with a look of genuine regret. 'Someone should have told you.'

Later, as I ran a hand through Megan's bubbly bath water, a string of uncharitable thoughts ran through my head. Like, for a start, if her father was serious about wanting to be considered to care for her, could he not make the effort to travel to the UK himself for the assessment? Secretly I hoped that, when it came to it, he wouldn't want to complicate his lifestyle with all the havoc that a toddler brings, but then I gave myself a silent telling-off. It was wrong to hope for failure, I knew that.

Feeling ashamed of myself, I lifted Megan out of the water and wrapped her in a towel. I knelt down on the fluffy rug beside the bath with her standing in front of me, all tummy and short legs. Before she was fully dry she wriggled away from me and leaned over the bath, trying to reach her toys. I marvelled at her tiny bottom and narrow back. She looked too tiny to walk, let alone talk as well as she did.

She wailed miserably when I dressed her in pyjamas, overtired from the hospital trip and her sore mouth. I rocked her to sleep, watching her small chest rise and fall. 'Rosie's here, sweetie,' I crooned, trying to ignore the heavy feeling in my chest. Whatever happened in the coming months, I was going to devote myself to making her as comfortable and happy as I possibly could. If, in doing that, I was drawn into loving her more, it just couldn't be helped: Megan deserved nothing less.

Chapter Twenty-Two

'Now, where is that little girl?' I mused exaggeratedly, putting my hands on my hips. From behind a large plant pot I could see Megan bunching her coat up in front of her, scratching her tummy as if her excitement was too much and needed rubbing away. I held my hands up in the air. 'I just don't know where she could be.'

The plant leaves rustled as Megan wriggled and squirmed, fists clutched to her mouth. Creeping theatrically across the grass, I arched my hands into claws, listening to the suppressed squeals punctuating her ragged breaths. 'I think she's around here somewhere,' I said, leaning forward and adding a growl.

It was all too much. 'Boo!' she shouted, leaping out and spreading her legs wide. I sprinted forwards and lifted her up, twirling her until she shrieked herself breathless. It was the end of March 2013 and the icy weather had broken, bowing out to one of the first mild days of the year. Megan had been poorly for the best part of a week with a heavy cold and an ear infection, so we were both making the most of being outside in the fresh air.

Every so often, as I chased her around the grass, my chest tightened with anxiety. I had missed a call earlier that morning from Hazel. She'd left a message to say that she had some news but by the time I called back, she'd left the office. Apart from regular updates from the contact supervisors when they dropped Megan home after her sessions with Christina, I hadn't heard anything from social services. I was eager to find out more.

Later that afternoon, wrapped up in thick jumpers, coats and gloves, the pair of us set off for the local shops. Halfway down the path Megan took a sharp breath and stopped abruptly. After taking a swift sidestep to avoid colliding into her, I leaned over, my face level with hers.

'What's wrong?'

'My sack-sack!' she cried, holding her hands flat and staring from one to the other. 'Sack-sack don!'

I suppressed a sigh. I had recently bought her a Peppa Pig rucksack and she loved filling it with random items whenever we went out. The trouble was, she also enjoyed unpacking it at inopportune moments, so it took forever to reach our destination. 'It's not gone, sweetie, it's inside. We'll get it, shall we?'

With rucksack in place she pottered at my side, performing little jumps between the lines of the paving stones, the bag bumping against her back as she skipped along. '*Whenever I walk in a London street ...*' I found myself reciting, the words echoing back to me from childhood. It was funny how that happened. I wondered whether Megan would chant the same poem to her own children one day.

'Again!' she demanded, when I reached the end, giggling every time I got to the bit about 'the sillies'. Every so often she stopped so that she could examine the moss growing at the edge of the pavement, the bracken tangled with weeds. She was still only 20 months but she loved walking, shunning the buggy until her little legs gave up the ghost and she could take no more.

We crossed under the railway bridge and passed a row of smart terraced houses, black wrought-iron railings bordering their tiled front paths. A black cat skittered out from behind a wide tub of azaleas and onto the pavement, pausing mid-step when it caught sight of us. Megan's face froze with intrigue. She crouched down on her haunches, her breath fogging the cold air. 'Tat,' she said, looking up at me with a smile.

'That's right. Cat.'

She groped at the space between them with her small hand but the cat leapt away. Megan toppled over, onto her knees. Bottom in the air, palms flat on the paving stones, she righted herself with a big effort and a grunt, spinning around to look for the cat whose sleek black body was weaving between a row of silver birches at the kerbside. Megan darted forwards as the cat dived across the road and disappeared over the top of a cobbled wall. She made to follow but I caught her sleeve. 'No. Cars,' I warned. 'Dangerous.'

Her face crumpled. 'Don,' she said, looking forlorn. 'Tat don.'

'Yes, he's gone to find some dinner, I expect. Shall we go and buy ours?'

She cheered immediately, skipping off ahead. Every time she heard the growl of an engine she ran back and slipped her hand into mine, pulling away when the road fell quiet again. She stopped dead at each passer-by, her eyes following them with forensic interest. Her face lit up whenever anyone engaged her in conversation, which they invariably did, even a menacing-looking teen wearing a black bomber jacket, his thin face framed with alarmingly gelled hair. 'Naughty man!' she admonished sternly when he dropped an empty bottle on the pavement and then kicked it into the debris beneath a hedge.

'Sorry, boss,' he mumbled with an embarrassed grin, eyeing me from beneath a block of black fringe.

Ever since Emily was born I had marvelled at how friendly people were when children were around. Whenever I walked along with a pram or a toddler, most people stopped for a chat or at least smiled and said hello. I remembered a detective friend of mine telling me that he was always confident of receiving a huge number of leads if one of the crimes he was investigating took place in a park, because dog owners and parents of young children tended to talk to each other more often than anyone else. Even if the witnesses he spoke to didn't know the name of the dog owner or parent, they could tell you the breed of the dog or the child's name, and were able to recall the smallest of details. The police were then able to identify further witnesses and eliminate people from their enquiries with ease.

We finally reached the shops half an hour later and, to Megan's delight, one of the miniature shopping trolleys was available. She ran to grasp the handle, her short arms stretched way above her head as she tugged it free. Using her whole body as leverage, she set about steering her way around the shop, stopping at almost every shelf to pick up obscure items we didn't need.

'Dried shrimp?' I cried in mock outrage, reaching in to the bottom of the trolley and pulling it out. Megan collapsed into helpless giggles and blindly plucked another packet from the nearest shelf. 'We don't need any tahini either, sweetie,' I said, giving her a warning stare, but it went in anyway. 'What is tahini anyway?' I said, pulling a funny face. Laughter bubbled up from her tummy and she convulsed again.

'Pease, Mama?' she asked when she'd recovered, so earnestly that I hadn't the heart to refuse her. The chocolate at the checkouts sent her into a scooping frenzy as well, and I had to stop her before she emptied the shelves. 'Want it,' she howled, shrugging off her rucksack and swinging it in a high arc over her head.

'I'm going to need help with all this shopping,' I said, pretending to struggle as I tried to lift the bits onto the counter. That was enough to distract her.

'Me help,' she said, leaning over the trolley so that her small feet left the floor.

* * *

Back home I began filling the sink with hot water. 'Me help, Mama?'

My heart sank. 'Oh, yes please, that would be lovely,' I said, preparing to get soaked. She ran to fetch the set of steps I'd bought for her and clambered to the top, tugging on her sleeves at the same time. 'Let me help you, sweetie.'

'Meggy do,' she declared, shooing me away. Her absorption in the task of pouring water from cup to dish fascinated me. My chest tightened as I watched her, assailed by the sudden conviction that Hazel was calling to let me know that Greg had been assessed as viable to care for her and that, at some point in the near future, she would be wrenched away. From then on I tensed at every sound; the washing machine filling with water, the fridge motor coughing to life.

Feeling hot, I pulled the sash window down to let in some air, breathing in the sharp fresh scent of outdoors. The noise from the street was a welcome distraction; the sound of children playing in the park across the way, river-bound gulls screeching as they flew overhead.

Jamie got home just after 4 o'clock and went straight upstairs with some of his school friends.

The telephone finally rang at 5 p.m., just as I was peeling some potatoes and Megan was playing with the skins. When I heard Hazel's voice I tried to sound casual, when really my heart was hammering. 'Oh, thank you for calling back,' I said, goose pimples rising and tingling on my skin.

'That's OK. I wanted to update you on Greg's assessment.' My throat tightened as I listened to her talking about her trip to Italy and the meetings she had had with him. 'It's been decided that his lifestyle isn't compatible with a young child. I think he came to the same conclusion himself, though he'd very much like to meet Megan. He's flying over next month and we're going to arrange for a meeting then. We'll take some photos for Megan's memory book, so she knows they actually met.'

'That's nice,' I said, feeling a rush of relief. 'Thank you for telling me.'

'That's OK. So I can't see any more obstacles now. You'd still like to keep her?'

'We'd absolutely love to.'

'Brilliant. Well, I saw for myself how well she's doing, so you have my full support. How is the little sweetheart? Is that her I can hear in the background?'

I smiled. 'Yes, she's helping me with dinner.'

'Ah, excellent. Erm, Rosie, since we've had a chat and I can hear that Megan's fine, can we log this call as a visit? I'm absolutely snowed under here.'

'Oh, yes, of course,' I answered immediately. Strictly speaking, social workers were supposed to visit the foster home once a month, but Megan was fine and there were no issues to discuss. I was only too happy to agree.

I put the phone down and gave Megan an extra-tight hug. At the time, it seemed we were one step closer to being able to keep her.

Chapter Twenty-Three

'Again, again,' Megan cried, as fine wisps of smoke rose from the candles on her Peppa Pig birthday cake. It was 12 July 2013, Megan's second birthday, and we were on holiday in a cottage near the seaside town of Whitby on the North Yorkshire coast. My brothers, Chris and Ben, had made the journey down with partners and children to help us celebrate Megan's special day, bringing presents that had been quickly pounced upon and torn open. The haul stood, precariously balanced, around and beneath the high chair she was sitting in.

'Oh, all right, just once more then,' Mum warned, patting the front of her dress. After a frisk, she reached into one of the deep front pockets and pulled out a box of matches. A brisk, no-nonsense sort of person who believed in administering justice the old-fashioned way, Mum's endless patience with young children always surprised me.

'Foo foo, Nanny,' Megan chirped by way of thanks. Mum had joined us for the whole week and Megan adored having her around.

The family erupted with affectionate sighs. 'Oh, Rosie, she's so cute!' my sister-in-law, Zoe, crowed, head tilted to the side.

'She's a big clever girl,' my mother agreed, smacking Ben's hand away as he reached over to pinch some pink icing. My nieces and nephews, ranging in age from 5 to 22, burst into another round of 'Happy Birthday' as they crowded around the dining table. Megan joined in, her mouth a wide O as she sang at full pelt.

I loved it when all the family met up, especially the inevitable commotion of having my brothers together in the same room. The banter flew between them and whipped the children up into giggling frenzies; the commotion providing a welcome distraction from worrying about what might be going on behind closed doors at the council offices.

I had tried contacting social workers in the adoption team on and off for weeks, to see if I could get my assessment under way. At first I was told that the social worker I needed to speak to – Veronica Harper – was off sick. I left messages asking her to call me when she was back at work and a couple of weeks later I rang again. Apparently Veronica was back at work but in training. Again I asked one of her colleagues to pass on a message asking her to get in touch but then another week or two passed without any word.

In June, after weeks of unreturned calls, I rang Hazel to see if she had heard any news. 'Not a sausage,' she had said, sounding uncharacteristically hesitant, apologetic even. 'I wish I could tell you more.' And then she added, for no reason I could identify: 'I can't fathom it any more than you. They're a law unto themselves.'

When I asked her what she meant she wouldn't elaborate. 'All I'd say is keep trying them,' she said, 'they'll have to get back to you at some point.' I decided to try and put their elusiveness out of my mind until after an Adoption Order was secured – no major decisions could take place until then – but throughout our holiday I had felt a hazy sense of unease, a nervy feeling in my chest.

My dad arrived for lunch predictably late, at 2 p.m., after the table had been cleared. Chris, Ben and I exchanged glances when one of the children ran to answer the door, all of us having registered Mum's fading smile. My parents had divorced years earlier and although Mum had always been keen for Dad to be included in family events as much as she was, she could still be a bit prickly in his presence.

Dad pecked the top of my head when he came in, then breezed past me into the cosy lounge. He was in good shape for a 70-year-old, long days doing outreach work for the church he belonged to keeping him trim. His salt-and-pepper hair had only recently started thinning and was now cropped close to his scalp, his glasses propped up on the top of his head. 'Hi, Grandad!' several of the children chimed, Megan launching herself at him as soon as she saw him.

'Hello, little one,' he said, picking her up and tickling her middle. She giggled and writhed and he slowly released his grip, letting her slide down his side to the floor.

'Look my bip-bops, Dan-Dad,' Megan said proudly, clasping hold of his trouser leg and lifting one of her feet to show him the flip-flops Zoe had bought her.

'Wow! Would you look at those?!' he cried, stroking the top of her head. 'Aren't you lucky?' It was funny to see Dad being so demonstrative with Megan – for much of my childhood he had been a remote figure, closed off from me. I can't remember sharing a single hug with him as a child, but he had thawed with age, and I think through his own difficult experiences in childhood, he felt a certain affinity with the children I looked after.

'Afternoon, dearest.' Dad tapped my mum on the shoulder and then hunkered down on the floor nearby. She tucked in her chin, cheeks dimpling with stiffness, lips pulled in a rigid line. She was appallingly, comically bad at hiding her feelings. 'Looking lovelier than ever,' he teased, throwing her one of his most charming smiles. Mum glared and shooed him away, but there was the tiniest hint of a smile at the corners of her mouth.

I escaped to the kitchen, setting a kettle on the cast-iron range and arranging some leftovers on a plate for Dad. By the time the kettle started to whistle Mum had defrosted, her laughter reaching me through the open door. I smiled reactively, with relief, as if I were 10 years old all over again. It took Dad less time to break through her frost these days, and he did have a way with people – he reminded me of Des, my supervising social worker, in that way. It was probably how he managed to attract so many newcomers to church on Sundays. Anyway, it was a relief to see them moving on from troubled times, oddly touching that they were still able to get on.

I took a tray through to the living room with a pot of fresh tea. The younger children, flushed with excitement, pounced on their cold drinks. Megan sat cross-legged between them, pleased to be part of the crew. When Dad had eaten and suggested a walk to the beach, she jumped up. 'Dan-Dad went beach yesterday,' she said croakily over her juice. She was remembering a day trip we had taken with my father the year before.

'We went to the beach with Grandad a while ago, you're right,' I corrected gently. It was so sweet, the way she referred to anything other than the present as yesterday, even if it were months earlier. My mum and Zoe exchanged smiles as Megan bustled around the place, collecting up essentials that she thought might come in handy for the trip – several felt-tip pens, a small empty cardboard box, the joker from a pack of cards, some empty DVD boxes and a corner piece from one of her puzzles.

By half past two we had reached the beach at Sandsend, Whitby Abbey nestled in the curve of bordering grassy cliffs. I held Megan's hand as we made our way down some wooden steps, conducting a mental headcount of all the children as we went. Emily and Jamie no longer needed me to keep tabs on them and all of the others, apart from Megan, weren't my responsibility, but it was an ingrained habit that was hard to break.

'Hot pot pickled bogey-pie,' Jamie chanted, holding Megan's other hand. 'All mixed in with a dead dog's eye. Scatter matter, spread it on thick –'

'Jamie, stop it.' He'd already taught her to say 'cool story, bro', whenever anyone spoke to her, which could have been worse – it wasn't unreasonable to hope that if a social worker overheard, they might see the funny side, but he'd also got her to shout, 'I want beer' with a thump of her fist on the table, which I thought was really stretching our luck.

'Freedom of expression, Ma,' he said with a faux pained expression. He swung Megan over the final step and onto the sand. 'Quit cramping my style.'

Megan squealed when she caught sight of the water, as if it had been months, not hours, since she'd last seen the sea. As soon as her sandalled feet touched the sand she ran ahead, haphazardly tipping out the contents of her rucksack while trying to remove her clothes at the same time. In the resulting tangle she fell sideways and shrieked a whine of frustration. One of my nieces bounded over to help as she flipped around like an angry, squealing turtle. When freed, she charged deliriously over the sand, picking up pebbles, shells and dubious discarded objects to stuff into her bag. 'Megan, no, not that, sweetie!' I called out, as she swung a greying wet wipe in an arc over her head. 'Dirty!' She dropped it and grabbed some old seaweed instead.

While the children tore around, crashing into each other and using bits of old driftwood for sword fights, the rest of us found a space along the wooden breakers. Ben removed his shoes and rolled up his trouser legs and Jamie, who lately seemed more drawn to his uncles than his younger cousins, did the same. When Ben sat down to read his newspaper, Jamie slouched beside him, intermittently tossing Maltesers up into the air and catching them in his mouth.

'No one can fall asleep that quickly,' Zoe complained a few minutes later, her husband supine, on the blanket she had set out on the sand. Chris's eyes moved with the give-away twitch of someone feigning sleep. 'It's just not humanly possible.'

Chris opened one eye a crack, caught Zoe's look and propped himself up on one elbow. 'OK,' he said with a sigh. 'What do you want me to do?'

'You could get your mum a deckchair, for a start.'

'Oh no, love, you stay where you are,' Mum said defensively. My mother was all for equality, except when it involved effort from one of her own sons. With the uncanny knack she had of transforming the most inhospitable places into a home from home, she bustled between us with Tupperware boxes full of sausage rolls, boiled eggs and cake. Each refusal drew a disappointed, slightly disapproving frown.

'We only ate an hour ago, woman,' my dad commented.

'Don't you call me woman,' Mum retorted snappily before trudging off to rummage through the rest of the bags. 'Drinks then?' she said, sounding exasperated. She pulled an assortment of flasks and cartons from her rucksack. 'Someone must want something to drink, surely?'

When Chris returned from the promenade with a hired deckchair, Megan downed tools and ran over. 'No, lovey,' my mum warned as Chris tussled with the frame. He turned it one way and then the other, his expression baffled. 'You don't want to get your fingers caught.'

'Chris looks like he's got it covered anyway, Meggie,' I said.

He paused, rolling his eyes over to me. 'A lesser man might lose patience at being mocked, dear sister.'

I blinked innocently.

'Adults?' Megan asked, tilting her head earnestly.

Mum smiled at me. 'Ah, bless her. Yes, just for adults. I've got old bones, that's why I need a chair.'

'But I big and tall and fat enough!' Megan insisted, her hands on her hips.

Chris leaned forward and tickled the toddler's tummy, then planted a loud smacking kiss on her cheek. 'Uncle Chris could eat you up,' he boomed, 'you're so gorgeous.'

Foster carers and their families weren't supposed to tickle the children they fostered – my family knew that, but with the little ones, they didn't seem able to help themselves. They also knew that we were supposed to encourage children to use our first names instead of family titles. I paused, chewing over the words: *No tickling! And probably best not to call yourself uncle either*. They hovered at the tip of my tongue but, feeling like a nag, I swallowed them, knowing they would fall on deaf ears anyway. I supposed that I should have been grateful that my family were so willing to welcome newcomers into our fold.

The next thing we knew, Megan was crying, holding one of her fingers up in the air. Force of nature that she was, she had dived towards the frame before I had a chance to stop her, catching her finger in one of the hinges. Mum reached her first. 'Oh, there now, it's all right, poppet. You've just got a black man's pinch. Let's pour something cold on it.'

Ben threw me a look over the top of his newspaper. Chris smirked.

'Uh, you shouldn't say that, Mum,' I said in a loud whisper, glancing over my shoulder to make sure we hadn't offended anyone nearby.

Mum had drawn Megan onto her lap and was pouring water from a small bottle onto her injured finger. 'There, that's better, isn't it, sweetheart?' She glanced up at me. 'Shouldn't say what?'

'You *know* –' I inclined my head meaningfully as Megan came over for a hug. I cuddled her to me, mouthing what Mum had said over the top of her head.

Mum blinked, uncomprehending. 'Look,' she angled her head towards Megan's injury, trying to add weight to her argument. 'That's what it is, isn't it?'

'Yep,' Ben said casually, turning the page of his broadsheet. He shook it out, ran his forefinger and thumb down the edge, folding it crisply. 'I do believe there's an article about it in the *Lancet* this month as a matter of fact.'

Rachel, his partner, slapped his leg.

'There you go, see –' Mum nodded with a satisfied look, but then her eyes narrowed. 'What are you lot grinning about? Oh, I see, so now you're all at it, picking up on every little word.' She reached out and snatched at Ben's newspaper. He clasped its rippling pages, scrunching the ends up in his hands and hooting with laughter as he lifted his leg against the onslaught.

'Mother, control yourself! Kids! Get Nanny off me, she's losing it!'

Within seconds the children stampeded en masse, all preparing to bundle.

'She's always had anger issues,' Dad contributed from somewhere over the other side of the deckchair.

'Don't you start, you so-and-so,' Mum snapped, but her eyes were twinkling. 'Downright rude, the lot of you.'

Megan, who had been curled up in my arms, suddenly sprang to life, tears drying on her cheeks. 'Bone!' she shouted. 'Bone's dinging!' She might have had hearing problems, but she always noticed my phone going off before I did, reacting with the same urgency as my mother whenever she got a call, as if lives depended on picking it up.

I grabbed my bag and walked a few feet away, Mum and Ben's light-hearted quarrel ricocheting back and forth as I pulled out my phone. The initial echoing two- or three-second silence told me the call was from someone in an open-plan office, and then I heard a crackly hello. It was Hazel. 'Sorry to interrupt,' she said, when I told her we were at the beach. 'I know you're on holiday but I thought you'd appreciate an update.'

'Oh yes, I would, thank you.' My stomach performed a flip.

'We've secured a Full Care Order and a Placement Order through the courts. All went to plan,' Hazel continued. Megan flip-flopped her way through the sand towards me, her eyes fixed on her feet as she shuffled along. She really did adore her flip-flops. 'They originally set aside four days to hear the case, but it was all wrapped up this morning. The judge has granted Christina, Greg and Jem letterbox contact twice a year, but that's pretty standard. So little one is all set for family finding.'

'Oh, that's wonderful news!' I cried, clasping my hands together. Megan mimicked my excitement, throwing her arms around me and planting a haphazard kiss on my skirt. I took her hands and she bounced up and down, her sandy flip-flopped feet on mine. Sudden loud laughter from behind drew her attention abruptly away and she ran off to join in the rumpus. Mum and Ben were still in the throes of a row, their jovial voices and those of the children converging so that it was difficult to pick one out from the other. 'I still haven't heard anything from the adoption team. Shall I give them a call, or just wait to hear?'

There was a beat or two before Hazel answered. 'Erm, you could give them a call if you like,' she said, but her voice sounded slightly strangulated, awkward.

I tilted my head, feeling uneasy. 'It's just that I expected to hear something from them by now. Are they very busy?'

There was a lull in the surf, the waves retracting and flattening themselves out over the shingle. At the edge of my vision, Chris was lifting Megan high up in the air, swinging her round. The other children were holding hands and wading through the water. I shielded my eyes against the sun as I watched them, holding my breath.

'They're always busy,' she replied after a second or two. And then she made a sound that conjured a picture of her pulling her lips in and rolling them slowly out again. 'Well, I'll leave you to it. Sorry to interrupt the party,' she added, before saying goodbye.

When everyone had gone their separate ways and the evening closed around us, I left Mum with the washing-up and gave Megan a bath. Hazel's words resounded in my head as I wrapped Megan in a towel and cuddled her dry, my earlier twinges of doubt fortifying into a definite sense of anxiety. By the time I went into the room I was sharing with Megan a couple of hours later to check on her, I was in full-on fretting mode.

She had fallen asleep on her tummy, knees tucked up beneath her and Dogger in the small space in between so that her bottom was high in the air. Gently, I eased the soft dog out and tucked him in beside her. Her wispy hair was damp at the forehead and I stroked it back from her peaceful face, kissing her on top of her head. 'Night night, sweetheart,' I whispered.

Deep down I think I knew then that something had changed. I just had no idea what it was.

Chapter Twenty-Four

'I have some excellent news for you,' Veronica Harper trilled over the telephone two weeks later. It was a drizzly morning towards the end of July, and I'd been calling the adoption team almost every day for the last fortnight, trying to find out what was going on. 'We've found the ideal match for Megan.'

Her words slithered around my head in slow motion, tightening around my chest. I listened silently as Veronica went on, so shocked by her announcement that I only caught a few words – 'married', 'professional', 'no other children'. I stood still, my free hand falling slack as I tried to absorb this new information. When the social worker fell silent, all I could do was parrot her. 'Ideal match?' My stomach lurched and my head was swimming. I felt giddy and sick.

'Yes. Mirella and Francis have been on our waiting list for a while, so I was thrilled to be able to tell them about Megan.' Veronica's voice was crisp and clear-cut; plummy, my mother would have said. 'They're affluent and well connected, and they can't wait to meet her. Of course they'll have to sit before a matching panel before that can happen, but I don't anticipate any significant objections.'

Disorientated, I gave my head a little shake. 'But what about us?'

'Hmmm?' Veronica warbled. She sounded vague, although I got the distinct feeling she was being deliberately evasive. I was pretty certain she knew exactly what I was talking about; she must have – I had written to the adoption team almost a year earlier, in late July. And what about all the calls I had made over the last few weeks, all the messages I had left?

'We asked if we could be considered,' I said, as calmly as I was able to.

'Oh yes,' she returned, with a flippant, condescending little scoff. 'Someone did mention that. Listen, if I had a penny for every foster carer who wanted to adopt the baby they'd been minding, I'd be able to give up my day job. I'm afraid we do have some carers who can't help blurring the lines between the professional and the personal.'

Minding?! So for two years all I'd been doing was 'minding' Megan? I felt a surge of annoyance at being so casually dismissed. Then again, I should have been used to it. Being a foster carer, like being a mother, was a low-status occupation. Some people saw the value in it, but certainly not all. Not that I was complaining – the rewards were far richer than almost any other job I could think of. But Veronica must have realised that the news she was imparting would be upsetting for us. I couldn't help but feel it was a bit insensitive to drop such a bombshell over the telephone.

I looked over to where Megan was playing. In the process of trying to insert a block of Duplo into her navel, she felt my gaze and looked up, smiling. A wave of determination rippled through my stomach. Megan wasn't just marking time – this was her home. 'She's very happy here,' I said, trying to project a resolute tone.

'I would hope she is,' Veronica said in a rather pious voice. 'Providing a happy environment is the least we expect from our foster carers. But foster care is a temporary arrangement and now Megan is ready to move into permanence. What I'd like you to do for me,' Veronica said, trying to sweep my objections away with a note of finality, 'is record some video footage of Megan playing with her toys or involved in some other activity. Try to find a time when she's most relaxed and –'

'I would still like to be assessed,' I said, firmly cutting in.

There was a pause. A slight, almost imperceptible groan. 'And we would welcome your application to adopt,' Veronica returned with equal firmness. A hard edge had crept into her tone. 'But not for Megan.'

My pulse thudded in my chest, urging me to object. 'That doesn't make any sense. She's already *here*, settled and happy.'

'And as I've said, we've found an ideal match for her.'

'But *we're* ideal for her!' I was beginning to lose my composure.

'Look, I understand why you'd feel a bit protective towards her. I suppose you're bound to after –'

'How can you say we're not a good match for her when you've never even met us?' I interrupted again.

'We don't encourage foster carers to adopt. We'd have no one left to foster if all our carers kept the children they were looking after.'

'That seems like arbitrary logic to me.'

'She'll be set up for life,' Veronica snapped, her first words overlapping my last and stopping me in my tracks. 'Do you really want to take that away from her?' I hadn't looked at it like that. My free hand strayed to my cheek and I sank down onto the sofa. Megan looked up curiously and came over, holding her arms out. I felt a pain in my throat as I hugged her tight. 'We have protocols and procedures for adoption, Rosie. It would be grossly unfair of us to let someone bypass all of that.'

My hands were still trembling when I put Megan to bed that night. 'No, Mummy, not that one.' Megan pointed firmly to one of the Alfie stories by Shirley Hughes. 'Want that one,' she said, her bottom lip rolled out in a determined pout.

'But I thought you might fancy a change,' I said, holding up *The Hungry Caterpillar* and raising my eyebrows invitingly. I could already recite every line of *Alfie and the Birthday Surprise* by heart. I wasn't sure how many more times I could take.

'No,' she said in an exasperated tone, shaking her head most decisively. 'Don't like change. Want Alfie one.'

My stomach rolled at the innocent comment. She was unbearably unaware of the turmoil that lay ahead, fragile and powerless. How would she cope with being torn away from all that was familiar? And how would the rest of us bear to let her go? It was too horrible to think about.

When the story was over I tucked her quilt around her chin and sat on the floor beside her bed, watching her face as her breathing slowed and she drifted off to sleep. I touched her cheek with the pad of my thumb and kissed the top of her head, hardly able to believe that she might be leaving us.

'Bugger that,' was my mum's brief response when I went downstairs and called her. 'You've always been too soft. You let people walk all over you. There are some things worth fighting for, and that little girl is one of them.'

Peggy was pretty much of the same mind. 'Oh yes, I know Hazel all right,' she said scathingly, when I called her at home. After the investigation, which had taken months to complete, Peggy had been exonerated and returned to work. Uncomfortable in the same role, though, she had transferred to work with the 14-plus team, who oversaw teenagers in care. She was a hit with the youngsters, by all accounts, who seemed to respond to her bluntness with a sort of mystified hilarity. 'Bends with the wind that one. She's pleasant enough to talk to, but she likes a quiet life.' I pictured the social worker's lips narrowing with distaste. For someone like Peggy who spoke her mind, there were few less appealing traits.

Emily and Jamie were out with their father and Tammy, so when I put the phone down I pulled on my coat and went straight into the garden, seizing the moment of quiet. The rain had stopped hours earlier, but the path leading to our shed and the shrubs along the ivy-covered wall still glistened and shone, the air filled with the soft, damp fragrance of late evening. Apart from early mornings, twilight was the only time of the day when there were no demands on my time and I loved sitting down with my last tea of the day, watching the setting sun and the hopping, chattering birds.

Sitting in my wicker chair, I tried to view the situation from the only perspective that truly mattered – Megan's. What the rest of us felt was irrelevant. It was Megan's future at stake and if we loved her, we owed it to her to put our own feelings aside. I ran through the earlier conversation with Veronica in my mind. It sounded as if the couple she mentioned had a lot to offer Megan, materially at least. To my mind though, love was far more important than anything else. As far as I could see, the choice was simple: stay with a family who adored her, or move on to an unknown future. The odds had been stacked against Megan from the moment of her conception, but despite all of that, she was happy and secure and developing brilliantly. While I could never be described as a high-flyer or well-heeled, I had a wonderful family to share with her and I loved her like my own daughter. Surely those were riches worth fighting for?

Across the garden, the pale light of the moon blended with the streetlamps' amber glow, making small patterns that danced on the path. I watched the light move and change, my mind flitting one way and then the other.

By the time I went to bed I had reached a decision – I wasn't going to give up on Megan so easily. The choice I had made didn't sit comfortably with me though, and I slept uneasily that night. Veronica's comments about taking opportunities away had pricked my conscience, and every time I woke, her words played on my mind.

Chapter Twenty-Five

At the sound of the doorbell my heart jumped into my throat – I could feel it thudding against my chest as I walked through the hall. Pausing for just a second at the mirror, I turned my head quickly from side to side in a last-minute check of my appearance, tucking a few stray blonde curls behind my ears. It was a week after the phone call from Veronica and I'd spent the first few days of August dashing manically around the house and garden, polishing, vacuuming and fixing. I could virtually see my face in the draining board. There wasn't a shrub that hadn't been pruned, nor a surface that wasn't bright and gleaming.

My brother, Chris, had popped over early that morning to fix the garden gate that had been hanging from one of its hinges. 'You worry too much,' he had said, as I tried to hurry him along. 'What on earth do you think I'm going to say to them?' Chris had a heart of gold, but he was prone to coming out with witticisms that not everyone appreciated. I wanted him out of the way before Veronica arrived.

'No, that's quite all right,' Veronica responded a few minutes later, after I'd offered to make her a drink. Around 40 or so, she was a thin woman dressed smartly in a grey shift dress, an expensive but restrictive-looking jacket and black wedge-heeled shoes. Her hair was dark and shiny, styled in a short bob with a harsh centre parting. There was a certain gloss to her, an impenetrable glaze that was difficult to warm to. 'I don't want to put you to any trouble.'

She crossed her legs at the knee and sniffed delicately, her eyes roving discreetly around our living room from her position on the sofa. My eyes followed hers, and I tried to imagine what she might be thinking as I took in the ingrained juice spills on the carpet, the odd crack in the paint on the walls. Our house was far from immaculate, but it was a happy place to be. I hoped that the superficial scars it bore might offer Veronica a sense of the challenges we had experienced with some of the children who came to stay with us, and the joys of watching them heal.

'Hazel?' It had been a surprise to find Megan's social worker on the doorstep beside Veronica. I hadn't expected her to come along for the interview as well.

'I'm fine actually, Rosie,' she said, with a brisk shake of her head. Sitting with stiff composure a foot or so away from Veronica, her hands were clasped tightly over the handbag in her lap. I wondered if there had been a disagreement between them on the journey over – the undercurrent of tension between them was palpable, and there was no trace of the playfulness of Hazel's last visit, even though Megan was playing with her train set just a few feet away from where she sat. Apart from a brief hello, there had been barely any interaction between any of them.

'OK,' I said quietly. Something definitely wasn't right. There was an undertone; something I wasn't quite getting.

'So, as you know, Rosie, we've been checking through our register of adopters within the borough, and we've managed to identify the perfect family for Megan. We're very pleased because sometimes when we're family finding we have to search much further afield for a good match.'

My chest tightened. I frowned. This was supposed to be a visit to assess my own suitability, but Veronica clearly still had her own rigid agenda in mind. 'But what about my own application?'

Veronica gave me a tight, patient little smile. 'As I said a week or so ago, we're not in the business of allowing foster carers to pick and choose permanent families for our children. That responsibility lies with us, and we've managed to find a couple who would be ideal for Megan. They're very successful. They live in a beautiful house with substantial gardens in a lovely suburb just 30 miles from here. It's idyllic, Rosie,' her voice softened and she fixed her cool blue eyes on me. 'I know you want the best for Megan. We do too, I can promise you that. And we're very experienced in matching the right children with the right families.' She inclined her head and gave me a superior little smile. 'We rarely get it wrong.'

I glanced at Hazel but her eyes skittered over me, refusing to meet my gaze. I knew what that meant – their decision had already been made. Once that thought had wormed its way into my head it was impossible to get it out and, I'm afraid, from that moment I lost my composure. The insides of my cheeks became so dry that when I spoke, my voice sounded croaky. 'But that doesn't necessarily mean she'd be happier there than here,' I said, although my voice had lost some of its conviction. Was it fair to jeopardise a life of privilege for Megan, just because we loved her?

Veronica looked at me narrowly. 'Tell me why you want to keep Megan. What's special about her in particular?' Her expression was inscrutable but there certainly wasn't any warmth in her gaze, or in the way her eyes ran around the room. And her earlier thin smile was nowhere to be seen.

'Well, she's lovely,' I said weakly. 'Wonderful.'

Veronica inclined her head, patronisingly I thought. 'Yes, most toddlers are adorable, aren't they? But what is it that marks Megan out as special to you?'

Choked and feeling under pressure, I couldn't answer immediately. I glanced at Hazel for support. Her eyes flicked towards me, but then she looked down at her lap. Her reserve stung me far more than Veronica's polite but barely concealed disapproval.

'Not to worry,' Veronica said, regarding me with a cool smile, although there was a hint of triumph in her gaze as well. I opened my mouth to speak, my mind suddenly bursting with thoughts of what made Megan so precious, but Veronica swiftly changed the subject. 'Do you have much of a mortgage here? Of course, we scrutinise the finances of all our adopters to make sure they're secure.'

I felt my cheeks reddening. I hadn't thought of that. 'I don't have a mortgage,' I said, sounding defensive, closed off. 'We're renting at the moment. But I'm in the process of trying to arrange one though.'

She looked at me askance. 'Really? So you don't own a property at all?'

My fear intensified. It seemed that things might really go against us after all. To my horror, I felt close to tears. I didn't answer for a moment, trying to recover. 'Not yet. But as I said, I'm saving for a deposit and looking to see what's around –' my voice faded away. Evidently uninterested in my plans, Veronica's eyes had begun to wander. I realised for definite, then, that the meeting wasn't about assessing my own suitability as an adopter at all. It seemed that the visit was more about trying to dissuade my interest so that Veronica could proceed with her own plans than any genuine attempt to get to know me.

The social worker gave a slight cough and covered her lips with the back of two fingers. 'Excuse me,' she said, swallowing. With each shift holding the potential for any number of complex and possibly harrowing situations, I supposed that some social workers might fake a cool exterior, simply as a way of getting through the day. Distancing themselves or nurturing a particularly black sense of humour were perhaps the only ways to stay sane. At least, that's what I told myself at the time. 'Rosie, it's obvious that you love Megan, but you really shouldn't have let yourself become so attached. Your job was to provide care, not love.'

She paused, her eyes gaining a calculated sheen. 'Look, I understand that she's settled here, but after a few weeks in her new home she won't even remember you existed.' I should have challenged her, put my own case across more firmly, but I was so upset that I didn't have the heart.

'We have much better options open to us, to be absolutely honest with you, Rosie. You have no partner, no home of your own and no secure income. Taking another child on under those circumstances strikes me as somewhat foolhardy,' she said. The corners of her lips curved upwards in a haughty smile as she looked away and snapped her folder shut. I think she knew she was making some headway. And then she put her folder to one side, her hand still pressed on the top when she fixed me with a cool stare. 'Some might say a bit selfish even.'

I felt a fresh jolt in my chest. My cheeks coloured with a fresh rush of heat, my eyes pricked with tears. Veronica opened the bag beside her and tucked her folder away, presumably preparing to leave. I couldn't believe it. They had barely asked me anything about myself, apart from making such an issue of me not owning my own home, their implication being, what? That because I didn't own my own home, I wasn't as worthy an adopter as those who did?

I tried looking at it from different angles to see if I could follow Veronica's line of reasoning. She made it sound as if it was preposterous for someone in my position to even consider adopting, when there were better options for Megan elsewhere. But better by whose yardstick, I wondered. And on what grounds were they basing their assumptions? I couldn't see how there was any way that Veronica could be sure that leaving us was in Megan's best interests. Did richer equate to better? The couple sounded as if they were successful professionals, but did that automatically make them nicer people? Better parents?

Of course, social services needed to know all about me if I was to be considered for such an important role, but what relevance did home ownership have on my ability to provide a stable, loving home? I was willing to be open about my life. I certainly had no secrets, but trying to be candid with someone who was so openly critical was difficult. Being misjudged was hard to endure as well. I felt irritated with myself for letting my emotions show, disappointed that I hadn't been able to maintain an air of cool professionalism. And at that moment, in perfect accordance with Sod's Law, Megan gave up playing with her trains and began tugging at my top. 'Play, Mummy. Play me.'

'I will in a minute, honey. Let's get you some colouring pens out, shall we?'

Megan declined, smacking the proffered pens from my hand. 'No want them. Want *Bug's Life*! You be Hopper. I be, um,' she tilted her head, forefinger tapping her bottom lip, 'I be Atta.'

Recognising the mischievous glint in her eye, the one that was almost impossible to distract or mollify without major fall-out, my heart sank. Within seconds she'd be purple, prostrate and quite possibly throwing up. I cast

Hazel and Veronica an apologetic smile and made a last-ditch attempt at negotiation. 'Tell you what,' I suggested soothingly, trying to pull the toddler onto my lap. 'You go and find the timer, set it on number ten, and we'll play *Bug's Life* very soon, OK?'

Megan wriggled away and knocked over the pile of books Emily had left on the floor beside her chair. 'Megan, come here, love,' I cajoled, as small whirls of dust that had been trapped under the pile escaped and snaked across the floor.

'Look!' she shrieked, delighting in her own misadventure. She rolled over in the mess, trying to catch the motes floating above her. Initially her antics struck me as funny, but when I caught Veronica's narrow-lipped expression I grabbed Megan's hands and pulled her to her feet. Small clumps of dust dangled from her dress. 'Urgh, yuk!' she said, her mouth twisting in disgust as she angled her head to get a better view. 'Dirty!' She giggled when I tried to brush her down, running away.

'She's a pickle,' I said, with a nervous laugh. Veronica gave me a thin smile back and then glanced at Hazel. A look passed between them, one I couldn't read. My heart twisted as they gathered their things.

I stood up half a second after them. Veronica offered me her hand. I took a firm hold, but her own cool fingers closed weakly around the back of mine. 'It's been nice meeting you, Rosie. I'm glad to have had the opportunity to explain our rationale in person.'

Once again I was wrong-footed. I hesitated for a moment, rocking back on my heels. And then I forced a confident tone. 'Yes, and I do understand your position,' I said, trying my hardest to maintain eye contact, 'but I would still like to be considered for Megan.'

She pressed her lips together, the lines of disapproval at the sides of her mouth deepening. Her gaze hardened, and suddenly I got a sense of what it must be like for birth parents, being scrutinised, being judged. 'Very well. We'll let you know our decision shortly,' she added stiffly, her voice high and tight. She folded her arms across her chest. Her jacket strained at the elbows. I nodded, but glanced at Hazel instead. I've never coped well with pretence, and by then I was finding it hard to even look at Veronica.

Hazel gave me a genuine, apologetic smile. She readjusted the straps of her handbag, hoisting it so high up onto her shoulder that it almost touched her ear. 'Bye bye, Megan,' she said softly, arching her head into the living room. 'Take care, Rosie.'

For a second, as they walked down the path, I was tempted to run after them with a definitive list of Megan's attributes. I wanted to tell them that I loved everything about her: her impulsiveness, her sense of fun and crazy lack of fear. I loved the way one of her eyes would drift inwards when she was tired, and that she refused to go to sleep until I had acted out the scene from *Peter Rabbit* where the poorly bunny trudges home to Mother Rabbit and she tucks him into bed with some camomile tea. I loved to watch her run, her short hair flying out as she went, and, sometimes, when she was really absorbed in a task, I would sit behind her, revelling in the glorious sound of her tuneless humming. I even loved the way she screamed when she went into meltdown, her emotions scrapping and colliding until she dissolved flat on the floor, furious and inconsolable.

I loved her with all my heart. I just wish the words had come to me when I needed them most.

Chapter Twenty-Six

'So, if you were an animal,' our Avoiding Allegations course tutor said, smiling invitingly as she cast her eyes around the room, 'what would you be and why?' Wiry in tight corduroy leggings and a fitted blouse, Natalie paced slowly around the 20 or so carers sitting in a horseshoe shape around her, tapping the end of a permanent marker on her leg. 'Come on, don't be shy,' she entreated, as if we were all secretly tripping over ourselves to join in and only collective timidity was holding us back.

Several of the attendees shifted in their seats and tried to avoid catching Natalie's gaze, myself included. After a few seconds of silence I risked a furtive sidelong glance at the carer next to me, a heavily built woman who had introduced herself earlier as Hyacinth. She rolled her eyes at me and sucked some air through her teeth. 'Oh Lordie,' she half-sang in a heavy Caribbean accent, her big hair hardly moving as she spoke. 'I love de kiddies, but I outgrown 'dis sort of game long ago.' She let out a loud chuckle. 'What about you?'

'With you there, Hyacinth,' I whispered, trying to deflect the attention she had drawn by staring down at the floor. The carer clutched my forearm and held on while she bellowed another laugh. I made up my mind to stay close to her for the rest of the session. It was the day after my meeting with Veronica and my mind was still broadcasting the lowlights in agonising little flashes. Veronica's twisted look of distaste when Megan decided to take a dust bath in front of her was one my mind felt worthy of prime viewing, each lingering replay making me shudder with fresh humiliation.

And Veronica's assertion that I shouldn't have allowed myself to become attached to Megan kept intruding on my thoughts as well. I wondered whether the social worker had her own children, although I knew it was irrelevant really – some of the best social workers I had known, Peggy for one, Des, too, were childless – but I couldn't help feeling that any woman who had held a newborn baby in her arms, even for just a short while, would surely understand that the compulsion to nurture was not so easily switched on and off.

Veronica had insisted that as a foster carer, I was supposed to provide care, not love. But weren't the two intricately interwoven?

If you imitate the actions of a mother often enough, there comes a crossover point, a moment when you realise you're not imitating any more. It creeps up slowly, in the early mornings as you plant a kiss in the child's sleep-tousled hair, and when it feels as if there's no one else awake in the whole country but the two of you. In the evenings, snuggled down together and sharing a story about Peter Rabbit or Winnie-the-Pooh. The moment comes closer each time you revel in a new achievement, every time you stick a plaster on a wounded knee. There are no fireworks accompanying it, no orchestra playing a poignant ballad as you tuck them into bed. But suddenly you realise that you would walk through fire for the child sleeping in your arms, just as you would for the children you're allowed to call your own. The moment came quickly with Megan, I have to admit, my mind fooling my heart into thinking that somehow she belonged to me.

In my own defence, she was adorable, and there was something special about her that compelled me to reciprocate the innocent love that babies offer so freely. And when I thought of the child Megan was and her warm, fun-loving, free-spirited soul, I was glad I hadn't done anything differently. If I had held her at arm's length, she might not have been the happy, sociable child she had become.

The scraping of Hyacinth's chair against the wooden floor as she shifted impatiently around dragged my mind back to the room. Disappointed with our lacklustre response, Natalie rubbed at the crocheted woollen hat pulled down tightly over her ears. Her long dark hair rippled, settling in two soft bunches down her chest. 'Come on, guys. You'll find the day is much more enjoyable for all of us if we each participate and give a little of ourselves,' she said, criss-crossing her feet as she walked sideways across the space. She stopped, pivoting on the heel of one sandal and then ran her eyes predatorily around the room. Her gaze settled on the woman sitting on the first seat nearest the door. 'Let's start with you then, shall we?'

The woman gained a frozen look. 'Ooh, erm. I can't think. I don't know. I suppose I feel a bit like a rabbit caught in the headlights right at this very moment,' she joked querulously. We all laughed. If the course tutors tended to take things just a little too seriously, the other foster carers I met on training days were often warmly supportive and humorous.

'You can move on,' Hyacinth said with a wave of her hand, when it was her turn to speak. 'I play enough games at home. I'm here for de certificates and de doughnuts, the rest you can keep. No offence.'

Her language was blunt, but I agreed with the sentiment. It was the sort of comment my mother would have come out with. To her credit, Natalie laughed lightly before settling her eyes on me. 'Rosie?'

'Um, an ant?' I offered, with as much frivolity as I could muster. 'Because I have a two-year-old at home and I'm forever running around after her and picking things up.' Once again, polite laughter rippled around the room. Feeling grateful for the support, I glanced around at the faces of my colleagues, wondering whether anyone else was feeling like I was – knowing they might have to face something soon and wondering how they were ever going to get through it. If anyone was, they were hiding it well, but then I supposed that they might think the same about me.

I could almost feel the tension flow out of the air when Natalie announced the ice sufficiently broken to move on. We all sank a little further into our seats, listening with horror and sadness as she told us about some true-life cases her colleagues had dealt with over the years – the baby intimately injured by her father, who claimed to have slipped while changing her nappy, the three young children who had been rescued by social workers from a tiny upstairs bedroom, where they had slept on a filthy mattress, a price list of sexual acts pinned to their door for outsiders to peruse and select from, the nine-year-old with broken ribs and gonorrhoea.

My usual reaction to hearing about such horrendous abuse being wrought on children was stomach-clenching fury, coupled with an overwhelming desire to do something good to counter the bad. Today though, as I listened to Natalie, the hairs on the back of my neck prickled. I felt so overwhelmingly sad that I pulled a notepad out of my bag and scribbled down some unrelated notes, trying to tune the details out. It was a relief when Natalie moved on to the potential pitfalls of caring for such badly damaged children. Dealing with the aftermath of abuse was something I felt much more comfortable with – the idea that, little by little, each one of us could help to soothe a child's pain.

'It's such a relief for us to deliver these children to the foster home,' Natalie shared, her brown eyes clouding over. 'Lots of people are under the illusion that being rescued from a life of neglect, ill-treatment or abuse at the hands of loved ones is going to be a relief for the child. But in reality it is simply another thing to add to their list of sufferings.

'Being torn away from their family, however dysfunctional that family is, does untold damage to the child. Sometimes of course, social workers have no choice, but as foster carers you have to appreciate that the children will suffer because of it. As some of you have already probably experienced, they're likely to react, and react badly.

'In some instances their daily experiences have been so traumatic that they find it difficult to distinguish between the present and the past. Some confuse the slightest affection as an overture of something sinister. It's our job to keep them safe, but it's equally important to protect ourselves and our families as well. That means staying dressed at all times when the child is around, staying out of their bedrooms unless a specific need arises to go in, and keeping the most detailed notes you possibly can, ensuring that your supervising social worker signs them off every time they visit the foster home.'

Towards lunch time I noticed an intermittent blue light flashing on my phone. My heart flew into my mouth when I saw the number of the missed call – it was the local authority offices – and a message had been left. When the others headed for the cafeteria, I found a quiet space along the corridor and dialled voicemail.

'I'm so sorry about yesterday,' Hazel said, her voice sounding muffled, as if her hand had been cupped over her mouth. 'I was in a difficult position, Rosie. Give me a call, will you please? I'd like to explain.'

The caller ID displayed was a mobile number, and I tried it straight away. As soon as Hazel heard my voice she gave a loud sigh, 'Oh, Rosie, I'm so glad you called back. I feel awful about yesterday, really crap.'

I snorted a laugh. 'It didn't go quite as I'd hoped.'

'No, and I'm really sorry I didn't say more, but I've been told in no uncertain terms that I have to take a back seat. I made it clear to Veronica how I feel about Megan staying where she is, but she copped the right hump on the drive over to you, telling me to back off and let her do her job. I thought I'd keep quiet or she'd only dig her heels in further.'

'Hmmm, yes, I did notice a bit of tension there.'

Hazel gave a laugh. 'Oh, it was awful. I made up some excuse about having something to do and got a bus back to the office. Talk about frosty.' She let out a breath and lowered her voice still further, so much so that it was a struggle to make out what she was saying. 'I couldn't come out and say so openly yesterday, but I want you to know that I do support your application. Veronica knows how I feel, but she doesn't take kindly to being told what to do.'

'So do you have any idea how the land lies now?'

'Oh God, after yesterday I haven't a clue. But I told them about it in the office yesterday, and they said Veronica's known for giving everyone a really hard time. It's nothing personal. And this might take you by surprise, but I heard from someone else that she really liked you.'

I sagged against the wall. It was such a relief to discover that I had an ally. Hazel might not be able to fully support me, but it felt good to know that at least one professional was on my side.

Chapter Twenty-Seven

After lunch a foster carer from a neighbouring borough came in to talk to the group about her own nightmarish experience of allegations. A small, rotund woman, with an open but tired expression, Carol had been fostering for over 20 years and was currently caring for a sibling group of four, two of whom had complex learning difficulties and anger issues. 'She was lovely,' Carol said of the 10-year-old who came to stay with her a few years earlier. 'She settled quickly and for the first few weeks she seemed perfectly happy. Then one morning she went to school and told her teacher that Mark, my 16-year-old son, had –' Carol stopped, glanced around the group and then grimaced '– well, she said that he had touched her inappropriately. Of course, she was removed from our care immediately. Her social worker turned up that evening to collect her things. When I tried to talk to her she refused to even look at me. She wasn't being funny of course, it was procedure. She wasn't allowed to discuss it. That's what happens when an allegation is made. All of a sudden you're a pariah. No one wants to know you.'

The room fell silent for a moment, and then Natalie asked, 'How did you cope, Carol?'

The foster carer blew out some air. 'We didn't really. I fell apart. If it weren't for the support from The Fostering Network I'm not sure I could have coped at all. I was so worried I couldn't even eat. But it was worse for my son, obviously. He was interviewed by the police, and I have to say they handled it sensitively, but he was terrified that no one believed him. And then a few days after the allegation was made he disappeared. Got up early one morning, packed a bag and ran away.' There was a collective gasp around the room. The feedback seemed to rejuvenate Carol. She nodded vigorously, taking on a more conspiratorial tone. 'Finding his bed empty that morning was the worst, most terrifying moment of my life. We heard later that day that the girl,' Carol glanced at Natalie, 'I won't mention her name to protect her identity, but she admitted to her new foster carer that she'd made the whole thing up. It wasn't her fault, poor child. She'd muddled past experiences in her mind, although there was a bit of jealousy there too, I think –'

'That's not unusual,' Natalie chipped in. 'When children enter the foster home they realise they're outsiders, which can sometimes lead to envy of birth children.'

Carol nodded avidly. 'She wanted my attention all the time. I think she resented it when I spent time with my own children.'

'So what happened to your son?' I hadn't meant to interrupt, but the question was out of my mouth before I could stop it.

Carol looked at me. 'We put messages on his Facebook page to let him know what had happened. That he was in the clear. We just prayed he'd see them and not do anything silly. And he did. He came home the day after the truth came out, sobbing with relief.'

The room fell silent, Natalie using the opportunity to drum into us the importance of maintaining detailed records and ensuring that other members of the family follow the safer caring rules. Carol's was a stark lesson, and one which really drove home the vulnerability of birth children.

It had been a draining day and by 4 p.m. we were flagging. Natalie had promised that she was going to wrap things up with a treat – I predicted chocolate cake but Hyacinth was doubtful. 'She probably got some other game up her sleeve, girl, isn't it?'

'What I tell you?' the foster carer demanded, when Natalie rubbed her hands together and asked us to push our chairs back and spread ourselves around the space in between.

'You'll enjoy this,' Natalie promised. 'It's a nice exercise to finish on, and one that will help us get to know each other a little more. It's a game called "Natalie says".'

Hyacinth let out a loud groan. I suspected that she might make her excuses and leave but she didn't. Instead, she followed me to the centre of the room. 'Hyacinth says, I'd very much like to throw something at de wall,' she said, leaning close to my ear but talking loud enough for anyone within a few square metres to hear. I giggled and squeezed her arm.

'So, I'll start,' Natalie said, throwing the pair of us a warning glance. 'Um, let me think. *Natalie says*, walk forward if you're wearing glasses.' Six carers took a few steps towards the front of the room.

Natalie smiled and bobbed around on her toes. 'OK, so, now, *Natalie says*, walk forward if you had toast for breakfast.' Several of us moved forwards, leaving only one behind – a pale woman with short grey hair and the name Nora on her name badge. Nora looked mortified but Natalie was beaming. 'Right, so as you can see, we have only one person left. That means you, Nora, get to be Natalie for a round. Come forward.' Natalie beckoned Nora to the front of the room and ushered the rest of us back to our original positions.

Nora, who looked relieved that her fate hadn't been worse, ran her eyes over the rest of us. 'O-K,' she began falteringly, '*Natalie says*, step forward if you're going to have a ready meal tonight.' The game continued in the same vein, most of us getting the chance to be Natalie. When it was her turn, Hyacinth shook things up a little. 'Natalie says, shuffle out de way if you're wearing red knickers like me.' Everyone roared. After several rounds, Nora ended up being the last person at the back of the room again. 'Oh no, I literally can't think of anything that hasn't been said,' she said, looking slightly panicked.

Natalie checked her watch and gave Nora a reassuring smile. 'That's OK, no rush.'

Nora's cheeks coloured. She looked exasperated. 'Oh goodness. OK, step forward if you're divorced.'

I glanced to my side and then stepped forward with a mock grimace. 'Looks like it's just me then.'

A few of the other carers laughed along with me and Nora clamped her hands to her cheeks. 'Sorry, Rosie,' she said with an embarrassed chuckle.

As soon as I got to my mum's house to collect the children, my phone rang. My pulse raced, wondering whether the adoption team might have already reached a decision. I pressed SEND, surprised to hear Natalie's voice in my ear. 'I'm so sorry about what happened earlier, Rosie.' Her voice was loaded with gravitas but I had no idea what she was talking about. 'Are you OK?'

I walked slowly up the path, running my fingers through my fringe. 'Yes, of course. Why wouldn't I be?'

'Well, after the incident earlier – I thought you might be upset.'

I stopped, frowned. Had she noticed that the case studies had upset me, I wondered. I didn't think so – I was an expert at appearing unruffled when I was feeling anything but. If it wasn't that, though, I had no idea what she was talking about. 'Upset? About what?'

'Nora's comment,' she said, concern threaded through her tone. 'I'm so sorry she brought attention to you in such a negative way. If you would like me to have a word with her –'

'Why would I?' I snapped, cutting her off in mid-sentence. It wasn't like me, but on top of my anxiety about losing Megan, it had been an emotionally draining day. At that precise moment, I wanted as little to do with social services as possible. Just for the evening, I wanted to completely switch off. 'Nora seems lovely. She didn't mean any harm, for goodness sake!'

There was silence at the other end of the line. 'I'm sorry, Natalie,' I breathed a moment later. 'I didn't mean to be so short. It's been a difficult few days.' I'm not sure if it was her sympathetic tone, or tiredness weakening my habitual resolve to pretend that everything was fine, but when Natalie asked what was wrong, rather than repeating the usual mantra, I told her exactly how I was feeling.

Chapter Twenty-Eight

'Guess where we're going today, pumpkin?' I asked, easing Megan's arm into the sleeve of her cardigan. Somewhere in the distance, church bells began to ring and my heart raced at the sound. It was a few days after Veronica's visit, and ever since then I had been on high alert, jumping every time the phone rang or the kettle whistled. It being Sunday, I knew there would be no news from the adoption team today, but still I felt anxious, wondering what the week ahead might bring.

Apart from attending the Avoiding Allegations course, I spent the days following our meeting close to home, waiting for the phone to ring. It felt wrong to venture far, somehow, in case I missed the news coming through, although I had a mobile phone, so there was no logic there. I held myself rigid, wound so tightly that my neck and shoulders ached. It was almost as if everything would be OK if I held myself still, without causing any ripples as I tiptoed through each uncertain day.

I kept imagining groups of social workers gathered around a table, analysing my personality, dissecting the responses I had given to Veronica during our meeting and shaking their heads at my unreasonableness. The thought made me feel sick with nerves. Hazel had said that Veronica liked me, but she had raised some obstacles in our meeting that could perhaps be considered insurmountable. One minute I convinced myself that she'd support me, and the next I was certain I didn't have a hope. In truth, I didn't have the foggiest idea what way things would go but I just wanted it over, one way or another. I wanted the stress to be gone. Megan sailed through each day of course, thankfully oblivious to my anguish and what the news would mean for her.

A surprise delivery late on Friday evening had lifted my spirits – a bouquet of flowers with a card from Natalie, the Avoiding Allegations course tutor, saying that she hoped everything worked out for me. My heart was warmed by her kindness and I suddenly felt bad for being so secretly disdainful of her party games.

For some reason my mind flashed to the news story about the baby who had been flushed down the toilet in China. Pictures of the infant, wedged tightly inside a sewage pipe, had been beamed around the world a few months earlier, the story making the front pages of almost every newspaper. What struck me most at the time was the number of people, both men and women and from all cultures, who were desperate to offer some comfort to the little one.

A small hopeful voice inside told me to trust in the system – Veronica hadn't seemed to warm to me at all but there was a chance she had been playing devil's advocate, perhaps in an attempt to test how strong my feelings for Megan actually were – but the undisciplined, negative corner of my mind kept throwing up renegade thoughts about us not being good enough to adopt. I tried to stay positive, but I found it hard to silence my doubts.

Megan bit her lip and cocked her head to the side. She loved these little games we played. 'Erm, park?'

I shook my head. 'No, not the park.'

'Where den?' she demanded, bobbing up and down.

'Try and guess,' I said teasingly.

'Nanny house?'

'Nope, not Nanny's.'

'Where, Mama, den?' She was staring at me intently, her excitement growing.

'Not Mama,' I said, waggling my finger at her. 'Rosie, OK?'

'Mama, Mama, Mama!' she chanted, her hazel eyes sparkling with mischief. She folded her arms tightly as if to underline the statement. 'Not Wosie, you Mama.'

I turned my head, looked at her mock sternly out of the corner of my eye. 'All right, I'll tell you where we're going, shall I?' She nodded vigorously, tilting her head and watching my lips in anticipation. I still wasn't sure exactly how much she heard of what I was saying and how much was guesswork. Her latest hearing test had revealed a slight dip in one ear, not enough to warrant a hearing aid, but there were times when she stared at me avidly, as if trying to decipher my words. 'We're going to a real live circus!'

'Circus!' she cried instantly, pulling away from me and spinning in excited circles, one sleeve of her cardigan dangling to brush the floor. 'Circus! Circus!' And then she stopped. 'Like *Bug's Life*?'

'Um, sort of,' I answered slowly, wondering whether she expected actual insects to perform on the high wire. 'Only this circus has people instead of bugs.'

Her brow furrowed in contemplation. 'Yay!' she shouted a few seconds later. When Emily trudged, sleepy-eyed, into the living room a couple of hours later, Megan immediately pounced on her. 'Going circus!' she cried. Emily laughed and spun her around. Both Emily and Jamie had agreed to come to the circus, something they wouldn't have entertained if it weren't for Megan. I think they loved reliving the excitement of their younger years through her eyes as much as I did. It was part of the joy of fostering small children.

Outside it was a beautiful day, the sky virtually free of cloud. As soon as we left the house I made up my mind not to waste any more time worrying – there wasn't anything I could do to influence the decision about Megan's future, and if she was to be torn away, it made sense to treasure every moment she was still with us.

We stopped on the way to pick up my mum. As we waited outside her house, Megan jiggled around in her car seat shouting, 'Go! Circus, go!'

Twenty minutes into the show, after a thrilling entree performance by four motorcyclists racing around a spinning metal cage, Megan sat enraptured at the sight of the trapeze artists as they swung from chains to a podium way above our heads. Her mouth fell agape as one of the Lycra-clad artists propelled herself from a high bar into a triple somersault, landing halfway across the space and dangling in mid-air, her hands clutching the ankles of another.

'That lady flied!' Megan shouted, whooshing her hand through the air in front of her face and then high above her head. Her face was alight with excitement.

'It's not as high as it used to be,' my mother whispered, sounding disappointed. 'They used to take real chances.' She still hadn't recovered from the news that there were no lions or tigers taking part. 'Rubbish, it wasn't cruel,' she'd insisted, after Emily had explained that the banning of wild animals from circuses was a victory for animal welfare campaigners.

'Course it wasn't,' Jamie chipped in. 'Nothing elephants love more than squeezing into an Eddie Stobart and whizzing up the M1, is there, Nan?'

We all glanced at Megan every time something exciting took place on stage, revelling in her excitement. I kept reminding myself about the futility of worrying, and the folly of allowing the unknown to spoil life's special moments, but as I breathed in the smells of popcorn and hot dogs and straw, and watched Megan's enrapt little face, it was so hard not to feel anxious.

I just couldn't imagine our lives without her beside us.

Chapter Twenty-Nine

The letter arrived two weeks later, a week before the end of August 2013. I had been desperate for news, but the sight of the envelope itself on the doormat rendered the reading of it almost pointless. Franked with the local authority's logo, its arrival told me all I needed to know. Had it been good news, there would have been a phone call; I convinced myself of that as I gathered up the rest of the post and accompanying pizza flyers.

Jamie was in the living room listening to music on his iPod, Megan was napping under her pink blanket beside him on the sofa and Emily was quiet somewhere upstairs, so I took myself off to the kitchen, a feeling of nausea rising in my throat. I didn't often pray, but I did at that moment. Instead of running my finger under the seal, I turned the envelope over and over in my hands, delaying the moment of almost certain disappointment. But as I slowly tore it open, part of me began to hope that my instincts were wrong. Would it not be easier for everyone to remain with the status quo?

Dear Mrs Lewis, the letter began, the paragraphs that followed swimming in front of my eyes. My hands shook as several words began to stand out from the rest – *pleased, satisfied, we will support you*. My heart hammered. I closed my eyes, took a deep breath and tried again.

> Dear Mrs Lewis
> Thank you for welcoming us into your home and allowing us the opportunity to get to know a bit more about you and your family.
>
> I am pleased to inform you that we are satisfied that you have the ability to meet Megan's needs and welcome the opportunity to assess you as one of our adopters.
>
> Please bear in mind that your position as a foster carer is no guarantee of success and therefore, the adoption must in no way be considered as certain. In the coming months you will be subject to a rigorous assessment, but we will support you through the process in any way we can.
>
> We will contact you shortly to arrange your first counselling session.
>
> Yours sincerely
> Veronica Harper
> Adoption Team Manager

A wave of pure joy ran through me. Paying no heed to Megan sleeping, I ran into the living room, waving the letter in the air. Jamie was on his feet in seconds. 'What have we won?' he cried, already doing a silly victory dance. I handed him the letter as Emily burst into the room.

She read it over his shoulder and they whooped in delight. Megan sat up, bleary-eyed and frowning. Seconds later she was on her feet and charging around, cheering at the top of her voice. I could never have guessed, in that moment, that events would very quickly take another dramatic turn.

Chapter Thirty

I remember everything about the day it happened. The way the wispy white clouds moved across the sky above the glass roof of our conservatory, the accompanying breeze caressing the dark-green leaves of the apple tree in our garden so that the fruit-laden branches swayed low, kissing the silver-white bark of the trunk. I remember hearing Emily, Jamie and Megan's voices blending together as they moved around not far from where I sat at the computer desk, the occasional shriek when one of them made Megan laugh.

The date was 29 August 2013 and it was just five days after the letter had arrived from the adoption team confirming that we were to be assessed as adopters.

Afterwards I cursed myself for checking my emails, wishing I had delayed the moment for just a little while longer, savouring the glorious, happy ordinariness of the day. Earlier we had driven across town to visit my brother

Chris, stopping off at a farm on the way home to pick some strawberries. Megan had gorged herself as she pottered, basket over her arm, and the sweet smell of the fruit lingered on her skin long after I had washed her hands.

Leaving her to wash the fruit in a bowl on her small table, I had switched the computer on with the intention of printing out some pictures from the CBeebies website for her to colour. As often happens, I got sidetracked, and ended up logging onto my emails instead. Among the adverts and reminders, one of them stood out.

It was from the adoption team.

Dear Rosie
On further examination of Megan's file, it has come to our attention that her birth mother has had contact in your home, a fact the adoption team has only recently become aware of. Unfortunately, after careful consideration and a full risk assessment, we feel that Megan's interests would be best served by placing her with an existing adoptive family in a secure location, somewhere she cannot possibly be traced.

I understand this may come as disappointing news to you and your family, but, as I'm sure you will appreciate, Megan's best interests and personal safety are paramount. We feel you have many attributes that would make you an excellent adoptive parent and welcome the opportunity to assess you on behalf of another child.

Please feel free to contact me if you feel there is anything you would like me to clarify.

Best

Veronica

It was only when I touched my hands to my face that I realised I was crying. At the sound of footsteps, I quickly clicked the mouse to minimise the screen and pushed the keyboard away from me. 'What's wrong?' Emily asked, coming up behind the swivel chair.

'Nothing,' I said, with a quick sniff. I couldn't face telling her right at that moment. I didn't know how to break it to her, for a start, and part of me wanted to deal with my own feelings before I shared the news with anyone else. There was no way I could put a positive spin on Megan leaving, feeling the way I did.

'M-u-m,' Emily said chidingly. 'I'm not a little girl any more. And I'm not as dumb as you think.'

I gave my eyes a brisk rub. 'Of course you're not dumb,' I said, angling myself away and pretending to tidy up the pens on the desktop while I tried to organise my face into a smile. 'I know you're not dumb.' I took a breath and grabbed the mouse, pulling the email back onto the screen. I turned to look at her. 'It's not very good news I'm afraid, sweetheart.'

'That's so unfair!' Emily said feelingly, as she read the message over my shoulder. 'They can't do that, can they?'

'She's not ours, love,' I said softly, wheeling the chair back and standing up. I slipped my arm around her midriff. I could feel her trembling with emotion. 'We let ourselves forget it, but Megan doesn't belong to us.'

Later that day, as we walked up the path to my mum's house, the edge of the curtain in her front room fluttered. She was expecting us. 'Here they come!' I heard Mum call out from inside, even though she lived alone.

Megan charged ahead. 'Nanny!' she cried.

There is something so comforting about my mother's house. Nothing ever seemed to change, from the clematis climbing up and over her door, to the peppermint smell of home cooking rising to greet us as soon as we walked into the hall. 'Hello, my little treasure,' Mum said, swooping Megan into her arms and kissing Emily and Jamie on the top of their heads. 'Well, would you look at those long faces,' she said as she ushered us in.

After talking to Emily and breaking the news to Jamie, I had called Mum to tell her about the email, but she was an expert at remaining cheerful, whatever was going on around her. 'All right, love?' she threw over her shoulder as she took Megan off into her front room.

'Right, I've got jam doughnuts just out of the fryer, or there's a bit of carrot cake left in the fridge. What do you fancy?' The sight of her soft, slightly translucent skin was always a comfort, the creases at the corner of her eyes that deepened when she laughed, the slightly reddened dent between her brows where her glasses tended to rub.

'Cake!' Megan shouted, lifting her top to reveal her tummy. She patted it with flat hands. 'Want cake!'

'Come on then!' Mum cried, holding out her hand. 'You'd better come with me into the kitchen. What about the rest of you?' she called out along the hall.

'Nothing for me thanks, Nan,' Emily said quietly.

'Me neither,' Jamie murmured. United in their gloom, they flopped down side by side on Mum's sofa. Emily stared into space. Jamie leaned forward with his elbows on his knees, chin rested in his hands.

My mum shuffled backwards into the room, losing her slippers in the process. 'Well, how about one of those lollies you like, the ones I get from Sainsbury's?'

'Not right now, Nan.' Jamie answered. Emily shook her head.

'Sod you then,' she said, sliding her feet back into her slippers. Jamie grinned. 'I'll make up some squash and they can make do with that,' she added as I followed her along her small hall. Framed photos of family members lined the walls, Megan taking her place among them. In the kitchen, the toddler was standing in front of the cupboards, waiting patiently. 'Mr Kipling do you, will it?' Mum asked, bending with a groan and pulling a packet of cakes from the cupboard.

Megan's face lit up. Remembering to say thank you without a reminder, she grabbed one, and then ran back into the front room. 'Sit down with it!' Mum called out over the rattle of crockery. She flicked the switch on the kettle then, standing on tiptoe, pulled two cups and saucers out of her top cupboard, lining them neatly on the worktop. They were from the same tea set she had used for decades, the rosebuds around the outside rim faded to a barely there pink. 'Right, now, I've been looking into it,' Mum said hurriedly, as soon as we heard voices starting up from the other room. 'And you've got rights.'

I leaned back against her small fridge. 'I know, Mum, but where am I going to find the money for a solicitor?'

She slid a glass door aside in one of the small cupboards nearby and removed a china teapot. 'I've still got that ISA I've been saving for a rainy day.' Above the hiss of the kettle, her voice caught. 'And it's definitely raining now.' She tutted, shook her head and poured some boiling water into the pot. After swilling it around and emptying the vestiges over the sink, she scooped up some tea leaves and scattered them over the bottom of the pot.

'Mum, that's lovely of you.' I think every member of our family had been offered her ISA at one time or another. I was amazed she still had anything left in it. 'But I think maybe they're right. Maybe it's not fair to keep her.'

'Balls to being fair,' Mum snapped. She hardly ever swore, but when she did, it shocked us to the core. 'Life's not fair,' she added, ignoring my dropped jaw. But her mouth had fallen slack and her eyelids drooped. I had told her what Veronica had said about security, and the risks associated with Megan's birth family knowing her whereabouts. Mum knew, once that idea was put into my mind, that I wouldn't be able to square my conscience if I continued with my application.

A minute or two later, Mum pressed a cup of steaming tea into my chest, her answer to all the world's problems. 'I wish I could do something to help,' she said with a sigh.

'Being here helps,' I said with a wan smile. And it was true. She couldn't change anything or make it better, but somehow, simply being close to her and knowing she cared, made everything that little bit more bearable.

At the irregular pad of heavy footsteps from the other room, we both turned around. Megan was running down the hall towards us, chocolate crumbs clinging to her chin. I handed my cup to Mum and crouched down on the floor, hands stretched out. Megan ran forwards and planted herself firmly onto my lap, wriggling until her back rested against my chest. 'No look sad, Mama,' she said, reaching out and forcing my lips into a smile.

That evening I sat alone in the garden while Emily and Jamie caught up on some back episodes of the TV show *Spooks*. From my wicker chair I watched as a light wind picked up tiny flakes of blossom and scattered them over the path. They glistened under the light from the moon.

Torn by my love for Megan and a compulsion to do the right thing, my thoughts spiralled and churned, first one way, then the other. I wondered whether to contact the adoption team again and tell them that I would give notice to my landlord and search for a new house immediately, but I knew they were likely to object. Even I could see that it wasn't fair to expect Megan to wait around for that to happen. Another part of me wondered how it could possibly be fair to wrench her away from all that was familiar: a secure home, her network of little friends and a loving, caring family. It seemed so cruel.

On the other hand, I suddenly thought with a touch of horror, perhaps I was guilty of not separating my own needs from Megan's. Was it my own feelings I was thinking about, more than hers? There was every chance that she'd be happier with a mother *and* a father's love. And anyway, I had finally been given a valid reason why Megan shouldn't stay with us, one that made sense – her safety was a priority and there was no way around that.

I loved her, but that didn't mean someone else couldn't grow to love her just as much. Emily and Jamie had always seemed happy living with just one parent, but they saw their dad regularly, and their lives were undoubtedly all the richer for it. If Megan stayed with us, I would be denying her the opportunity to be loved by two parents. Should I fight for the chance to keep her, or let her go? It was a near impossible decision to make.

By the end of the evening, with a heavy heart, I decided that it was my duty to stand aside and give her that chance.

Chapter Thirty-One

Once I withdrew my application, things began to move very quickly. With Francis and Mirella Howard's adoption panel date scheduled for mid-September, Hazel had arranged a one-hour contact session for Christina, Megan's birth mother, at the beginning of the same month – an opportunity for her to say goodbye. Contact sessions usually lasted somewhere between 90 minutes and three hours, but since emotions inevitably ran high for the parting families, social workers aimed to avoid prolonging the agony of the final contact by keeping it brief.

Hazel had also organised a meeting between Megan and her birth father, Greg, which would take place straight afterwards. Greg had flown into the country a couple of days earlier, seizing his one final chance to meet Megan and wish her well. Hazel told me that she intended to supervise his contact so that she could take some photos for Megan's life-story book.

Prone to over-identifying with other people, I woke that morning with a churning stomach and a lump in my throat. I could hardly imagine how Christina must be feeling. Her life was complicated and her problems had impacted negatively on Megan, but I didn't think she was a bad person. Whatever the circumstances (with the exception of sexual abusers – I struggled to find a shred of sympathy in my heart for them), the permanent separation of a mother and her child was profoundly sad, and my heart went out to both of them on that day.

Not that Megan was aware of what was about to happen, or at least, so it seemed. Whenever I got her ready for a session with Christina I told her she was going for contact, and for the last few months she had begun to refer to their time together as 'hay house', in honour of the little playhouse she loved in the family centre garden. At just over two years old, her understanding was limited and I was never sure whether she had any idea of who Christina actually was. During the sessions she referred to her mother as 'lady', though I had been told by the contact supervisors that Christina sternly corrected her, saying repeatedly, '*I'm* your mummy, not Rosie. OK, yeah?' I could understand her frustration at being sidelined, but once Megan's adoption became inevitable, it seemed futile, unfair even, to press the point.

On the day of contact Megan woke soon after 7 a.m., belting out the theme tune of *Balamory*. When I went to her bedroom she greeted me with her usual beaming smile, holding her arms out over the bar of her cot. My mind fast-forwarded to the moment of our own parting as she sat on my lap with her morning milk, but I wasn't going to allow my thoughts there, not before I had to. I held her extra close, pushing everything else firmly aside.

She was excited to wear the new dress I'd bought for the occasion – parents usually liked to take keepsake photos during the session, and I wanted Megan to look nice for her mum. After she was dressed she sat beside me on the sofa and I showed her the photograph album I had filled last night as a keepsake for Christina. Starting with pictures I had taken of her as a newborn baby in the special care baby unit and then continuing on through all her milestones; her first Christmas was included, our trips to the seaside, her birthday parties.

Megan's short fingers scrabbled with the pages, her breath ragged with intrigue. She loved seeing photos of herself, particularly those from when she was tiny. 'Baby Meggie,' she said, touching the pages, and then, patting her own chest: 'Big girl Megan.' I laughed, squeezing her into a hug.

Another picture she took delight in was that of Emily sitting on the beach at Whitby, the sun high over her head and Megan in the background, holding a baby crab aloft in her hand. I felt a tightening beneath my breastbone as we came to the last few pages of the album, knowing that our own story would soon come to an end. There would be few opportunities now for family photos, at least ones with Megan included in them. There would be no pictures of her on her next birthday, or as a four-year-old in her uniform on her first day of school.

At a little after half past nine I gave Megan's hair one last brush and stood at the window with her in my arms. Up until that day, I had always dropped her off at the family centre, a contact supervisor covering the return journey. But since it was Christina's last contact, Hazel had arranged for social services to transport both ways, in case Christina or one of her friends made an attempt at abduction – if ever there was a moment when a distressed parent might try something reckless, it was during their final session of contact. It had happened before and I knew security at the family centre would be heightened, just in case. For my part, I was relieved that I didn't have to witness their final hug; I had witnessed last farewells before, and the sadness of it stayed with me for days.

I saw Christina the next day though, at Megan's LAC review. It was raining again, but, eager to avoid bumping into Veronica outside of the meeting, I took my time searching for a place to park, arriving at the council offices just a few minutes before the scheduled start. It wasn't Veronica's fault that Megan couldn't stay with us, but for some reason I felt a lingering resentment towards her, probably because she had been the first to suggest that a new family had been found.

The receptionist directed me up to a small conference room on the top floor of the building. The air in the corridor up there was fusty, the carpet threadbare and so faded that the colour was unidentifiable; a greyish, milky fawn, like stale, cold tea. A few doors stood open to reveal mostly empty rooms, aluminium shelving abandoned in the corner of one, old, water-damaged books piled up in another.

When I entered the small conference room where the meeting was to be held, the first person I noticed was Alex Stone, a mature but wiry black man with a smooth bald head and brown eyes magnified by the thick-lensed glasses he wore. Standing at the head of a long oval table, Alex was shaking out a light grey overcoat, brushing at the suede collar with his free hand.

I had met Alex several times before and when he looked up and saw me he draped his coat over one of the nearby chairs and then strode over to shake my hand. Shunning the casual jumpers and cords popular in social work circles, Alex was dressed immaculately in a well-cut dark-blue suit and crisp pale-pink shirt, his tie a duskier, deeper pink. Still clutching my hand, he asked after Emily and Jamie, whose names he miraculously remembered, even though it must have been over a year since we'd last met.

Veronica met my eye only briefly as I skirted the table. I forced myself to offer her a smile, though I could only conjure a weak one. She nodded and smiled back, though seemed uncomfortable and quickly glanced away. 'We're still waiting for the child's social worker,' Alex said in a deep baritone voice as he took his own seat. 'She called to say she'd be a few minutes late. I plan to begin soon after she arrives. I haven't heard anything from the child's mother, but one would hope that she's on her way.'

Veronica gave a tiny, almost imperceptible snort. Annoyed, I glanced at her, but she kept her eyes focused on her notebook, her pen hovering above it. At the sound of a mobile going off, Alex lifted his hand in apology and left the room to take the call. Silence took over. Apart from the intermittent sound of car tyres on wet tarmac outside, there wasn't a sound in the room. I found myself studying the empty aluminium chairs dotted around the table and piled high in one corner of the room. They put me in mind of the riverside café near our home, where hot drinks and pastries were served throughout the year from a wooden hut by a hardy soul who didn't seem to notice the cold. I found myself wishing I was there now, Megan skipping around while I bought some pellets for the ducks (a profitable sideline for the tea hut), Emily and Jamie waiting for a bacon sandwich.

The sound of the door creaking transported me back into the room. Hazel came in first, a sodden umbrella hanging from her wrist by a handle of thin rope. Christina blasted in afterwards, following Hazel around the table and sitting in one of the chairs I'd been staring at. Christina's eyes ran around the room. I smiled when she settled her gaze on me. 'That got me here,' she said, banging her hand on her chest. 'What you did for me yesterday really got me. It was so nice.' She must have noticed my blank expression because just as the door opened and Alex re-entered the room she said, 'The photos.'

'I'm glad you liked them,' I said softly, as Alex cleared his throat. He waited for silence and then interlinked his hands, resting them on the dark-blue file in front of him.

'Thank you, everyone. I'd like to start now, if I may. I'm Alex Stone, Independent Reviewing Officer for this meeting today.' I remembered then that Alex was a stickler for following the proper procedures. There were only five of us in the room, but he asked that we announce our names and roles to the group, inclining his head first to Veronica. After Hazel and I introduced ourselves, all attention fell upon Christina.

She scowled. 'It's fucking obvious who I am.' It was an accurate reply, honest and succinct. Veronica looked up from her notes, nostrils flared.

Alex dipped his head. 'Indeed, indeed. And we're very grateful to you for attending the meeting today, Christina. May I call you Christina?'

'It's my fucking name innit?'

Unruffled, Alex nodded. 'Indeed. Precisely. Absolutely correct. Before we move on, may I say, Christina, that we appreciate this isn't going to be an easy meeting for you. That much is acknowledged by all of us, I'm sure. Your attendance will be recorded in the minutes, and when Megan is older, if she chooses to read her file, she'll know that you made an effort to attend.' His eyes lingered on her for a moment, but when there was no response, he moved on. 'The purpose of this meeting is to update ourselves with Megan's progress and discuss the plans being put in place to secure permanence for her, now that a Full Care Order has been obtained. Hazel, would you bring us up to speed in terms of our legal position, please?'

Hazel opened her mouth to speak but Alex lifted his hand. 'I beg your pardon, Hazel. May I just add, Christina,' he looked across the table to where she was sitting, 'that you have a right to call a halt to proceedings at any point if you hear something you don't understand. I will endeavour to explain, but if we can't resolve any misunderstanding between us, there are systems in place for you. I'll furnish you with the details after the meeting, should you want details of leave to appeal.'

Christina stared at him with the hopeless expression of someone who didn't have much confidence in anyone or anything, let alone the system. Was she right? I wondered. I was still hoping for someone in authority to overturn Veronica's decision. I may have disagreed with a few social workers along the way, but my faith in the department as a whole was still intact.

Hazel clarified the legal position – a Full Care Order meant that Christina had been stripped of her parental rights, and no longer shared responsibility for Megan's care with the state – and then went into detail about future contact with her birth family. Christina and Greg had both been granted two letterbox contacts a year, providing them with the opportunity of writing letters to Megan, which would be forwarded to her new family via the adoption team. Adoptive parents were expected to respond twice a year with letters of their own, and perhaps drawings or something personal from the child. As Hazel spoke, Christina stared around the room with slack-jawed disinterest, intermittently scrolling through her phone. 'Has the final contact taken place?' Alex asked, when Hazel eventually fell silent.

The social worker nodded. 'Yes, yesterday. And I have to say, Christina dealt with the situation extremely well.'

'What fucking choice did I have?' Christina demanded, though she spoke the words mildly, her attention absorbed by something on her screen.

'Well, you'd be surprised, Christina,' Hazel said, staring at the top of the young woman's head. 'You held yourself together for Megan's sake. Not all parents are able to do that. We were very grateful.' Christina looked up, snorted with disdain and lowered her eyes again.

'Indeed. Well done, Christina,' Alex chimed. She didn't respond. 'OK, so,' he turned to me, 'Rosie, would you tell us how Megan is doing at the moment, please?'

It was a task I had been expecting, but when I tried to find my voice, a lump rose in my throat. I waited a beat or two, trying to concentrate on the rain running down the windows opposite. It worked, and for the next five minutes I spoke clearly about Megan's day-to-day routines and the things she enjoyed doing, capturing the essence of her with no outward sign of the turmoil going on in my chest. Hazel's eyes widened when I told them that Megan no longer wore nappies during the day, surprised to hear that, even though I'd only introduced the potty last week, she was already dry.

Alex smiled warmly as I spoke. Christina looked up intermittently, and Veronica smiled insipidly. 'What you've said concurs with the report I've received from the paediatrician who conducted Megan's health-care assessment,' Alex said, when I fell silent. 'She seems to be doing very well.'

'Absolutely,' Hazel chipped in. 'She's a very happy little girl.' I might have imagined it, but there seemed to be an edge to her tone, as if she had a point to make.

'Indeed, very pleasing. Hazel, would you care to update the meeting on current plans.'

Hazel nodded. 'A Full Care Order was secured on 12 July. In line with procedure, Megan's file has been passed to the adoption team. They've identified several couples who might be able to meet Megan's needs, with one couple standing out as being particularly suitable. I'll let Veronica fill you in a bit more on that. Rosie, her foster carer, had asked to be considered, but the adoption team have ruled that option out,' Hazel said, pointedly again, I thought. Christina looked up sharply. 'In the interests of placing Megan swiftly into permanence, Rosie has since withdrawn her application.'

'I see,' Alex said, his eyes meeting mine. He looked puzzled, but Veronica jumped in quickly before he could say anything.

'We have a couple due to attend matching panel in about ten days,' she offered, without prompting.

'Yes, a-ha.' Alex placed his hands on the table. He stared at them for a few moments and then he fixed his gaze back on the social worker. 'Veronica, may I press upon you the importance of exploring all avenues when considering where Megan's best interests lie, not just those you may have originally had in mind.'

Veronica stiffened, taking on a haughty expression. A rapid exchange ensued between them, one that I was only peripherally aware of. I was busy praying for Christina to show some sort of reaction. Something was happening – her phone lay abandoned on the table, her fingers frozen above the keys. Her eyes were running around the assembled group and she was frowning with incomprehension. Come on, I thought. Please say something. When she looked at me I gave the tiniest shrug of my shoulders, raising one eyebrow just a fraction. It was a subtle incitement to action but at first it didn't seem to have any effect. Christina looked away. Then she gave a long, slow blink. 'What did you just say?'

Veronica had been addressing the group but she stopped in mid-sentence. 'I'm sorry?'

'Not you. Her.' Christina flicked her be-ringed forefinger at Hazel. 'What did you just say?'

Hazel's expression was non-committal, but I got the impression it was the reaction she'd been hoping for. 'Er, I was just listening to Veronica actually, Christina.'

'I know that. I'm talking about a minute ago, before she started waffling. What you said about her.' She flicked her finger at me. Veronica suddenly looked uncomfortable. She squared her shoulders as Hazel repeated what she'd said. Christina listened with her mouth open. 'You ain't serious. Is she for real?' she demanded, looking at me. I nodded but I didn't say anything, my lips pressed together. 'Who the fuck decided that was a good idea?' Christina scanned the faces in front of her, jaw hanging, though this time there was purpose in her eyes. They were blazing with fury. I felt a huge surge of affection for her.

For a moment there was silence, and then Veronica cleared her throat. 'We have a number of excellent couples who have been waiting for a suitable child,' she said, emphasising the pluralism. 'And one in particular who stand out as being –'

'Yeah, yeah, you said all that already. But that's her mum sitting there,' Christina interrupted, jabbing her forefinger at me. 'Or it may as fucking well be. It ain't me who got up to her every night when she was puking, was it? I'd have loved to have that chance, but 'cos of you lot I couldn't. So Rosie did it instead. And she always dressed her beautiful. Remember that pink tracksuit you put her in?' she demanded, looking at me. 'She looked like a princess in that.' I didn't think princesses were known for their tracksuits, but Christina could have come out with whatever she liked at that moment, as far as I was concerned. There was a valid reason why Megan couldn't stay with me – it wasn't Veronica's fault, or anyone else's, but after her initial disapproval, it felt good to hear Christina speaking out for me. I could have hugged her. In fact, in that moment I loved her – her husky voice, the profanities, the bizarre and random one-liners; I loved it all.

'So what you gonna do with her then? Dump her with strangers?'

Veronica lifted her chin, gathering her composure. 'Not at all,' she returned coolly. 'We're highly experienced at matching the right child with the right adoptees. As I said before, we have an excellent couple in mind for Megan. We think she'll be very happy with them.'

'Perfect couple? Fuck that,' Christina snapped. 'They could be divorced next year for all you know. Whereas she's already fucked things up in that department, so there's no nasty surprises waiting for her, you get me?'

I choked a cough at that, I couldn't help myself. I felt very close to giggling. 'I ain't being funny or nuffink, Rosie, but you know what I mean. Better the devil you know, ain't it? And I can see my girl is happy. She counted to ten yesterday, do you know what I mean? That kid's a genius. Only just two years of age and she counted to ten.' Christina turned to address the others, the sorrow plain on her face. 'I had to say goodbye to her, do you hear that? Yesterday, I had to say goodbye to my baby girl. I probably ain't never gonna see her again. Nearly broke my fucking heart, but knowing she's with someone that teached her to count, that makes it a little bit better, see? And I thank you for that, Rosie,' Christina banged her hand flat against her chest again, her eyes fixed on me again. The translucent crescents of tiredness beneath her eyes pulsed a faint blue. 'I thank you from the bottom of my heart, I really do. I just wish you could adopt me too.'

There was no guile in her. I knew that whatever she said could be taken at face value, and her sincerity touched me. I nodded, gave her a grateful smile, and then returned my attention to the aluminium chairs. I was close to tears myself, but if I'm honest, they were as much for myself as for Christina.

Chapter Thirty-Two

Veronica called two weeks later to let me know that Francis and Mirella Howard had been approved by the adoption panel as a suitable match for Megan. The news came as no surprise to me – like the panels held every three years to reassess a foster carer's approval, the outcome was usually a foregone conclusion, the relevant paperwork having been submitted to individual panel members weeks in advance – but when Veronica told me that the prospective adopters wanted to meet me, the full magnitude of what was about to happen really started to hit home.

'Would next week suit you?' Veronica asked coolly over the line. Megan clambered for the phone. Clutching rolls of my jumper in her hands, she scaled my shins and tried to get a foothold on my knees.

'Who dat?' Megan demanded, releasing one hand and swinging from me as she made a grab for the receiver. 'Me speak Nanny!' she shouted.

'It's not Nanny, sweetie,' I whispered.

There was a pained silence at the other end of the line. It seemed Veronica was getting impatient. 'The beginning of October?' she prompted. 'We were thinking the afternoon of the 4th.'

I felt a pang in my heart as I confirmed the time and ended the call. I knelt down and folded Megan into my arms. 'Love you all much, Mama,' she said, stretching one of her hands as high as it would go. I smiled. 'I love you all up too,' I said, kissing the top of her head. A rush of guilt swept over me. Abandoning my application felt like a betrayal of her, despite my doing it with the best of intentions.

On the morning of 4 October I forced myself to eat some toast while the others tucked into their porridge. Ever since Veronica had called about the meeting with the Howards I hadn't been able to shake the nauseous, swooping feeling in my stomach. Megan's adoption suddenly became all the more real.

Outside, the rain was falling in squally sheets and the house felt cold, even with the heating on. I rubbed at my arms, pulled on a cardigan, but when my mum turned up to look after Megan an hour later, I still felt a chill in my chest.

The storm had swept in before first light and as I drove over the iron bridge towards town the rain intensified, my wipers doing little to keep the windscreen clear, even at full throttle. Beyond the water, the old brick warehouses along the dock stood tall and ghostly, the clouds a cloak of battleship grey. Moody and invasive, the tide trespassed further up the banks than usual, turning the grass into green sludge as it plunged back into the murky water.

I drove cautiously, even as the narrow streets gave way to wider, tree-lined roads. The trees were almost bare, droplets of rain clinging to the last of the reddened leaves and forming a sludgy pool among the less hardy ones below. I tried to keep my mind from fretting by listening to the radio, but each song struck a chord with the situation and made my heart ache. The news channels were worse, endlessly depressing: migrants drowning off the coast of Italy, stark warnings of a second global financial crisis, clinics keeping quiet about parents aborting healthy but unwanted baby girls.

The act of walking from the car to our meeting place – a café in the park near the local authority offices – swept my nerves away. By then the rain had softened into a fine drizzle and the air was coolly distracting against my face, but when the café came into view, my anxiety returned with a vengeance. Visions of the couple made my pulse thrum faster and transported me back in time, to the day I met baby Sarah's adoptive parents for the first time. Being introduced to adopters was an anxious moment for foster carers, but within milliseconds of setting eyes on Paul and Kate I had been flooded with a sense of relief. I felt immediately at ease in their company, certain that Sarah would be safe with them.

They turned out to be the most generous spirited of people, so much so that they allowed us to see Sarah from time to time and kept in touch, sending us photos and updates on her progress at nursery. I just hoped that the strangers who would soon be caring for Megan would be as nice a couple as Kate and Paul. Thoughts of that special family kept me company as I crossed the grass. Outside the café, my pulsed raced. I took a deep breath and went in.

The three of them were sitting around a table near the far wall. Veronica stood as I walked over, a thin-lipped smile on her face. 'Rosie,' she said, with a handshake even weaker than our last. 'I'm so glad you could make it. 'Francis, Mirella,' the social worker swept her arm between us. 'This is Rosie Lewis.'

Francis and Mirella were sitting side by side on the opposite side of the table. Francis stood and shook my hand. Mirella remained seated but smiled warmly, so I just nodded towards her and returned the smile. Francis made little a-ha, hu-hum noises in his throat as we took our seats, evidently feeling the need to fill even the shortest of silences. Immediately I felt a connection with him; with his furrowed eyebrows and tight jawline, he looked as daunted by the situation as I felt myself.

Mirella, by contrast, appeared perfectly relaxed. Casually sipping her tea as I slipped my coat over the back of my chair, this might have been a casual business lunch, or even a meeting between old friends. She glanced at me over the rim of her cup, her deep-set pale-blue eyes interested, assessing. Slightly older than her husband, I guessed she was around 50 or so to his early 40s. She was wearing a tailored jacket over a black roll-necked jumper, her long, tasteful necklace matching the small studs in her ears.

'Tea or coffee?' Veronica asked, her head cocked to one side. I still found it difficult to look at her, even more so now she was smiling. She gave a small nod of her head towards the centre of the table, where a glass carafe of coffee and a large silver teapot stood. 'I ordered both.'

I knew that Veronica probably expected me to be emotional, so I determined not to be. I didn't want to follow the narrative she had set out for me. Composing myself, I thanked her and reached for the teapot, making bright small talk as I poured the hot liquid into a cup. Francis responded, hesitantly at first, telling me that they only lived about 30 miles away. As he spoke he pushed the sugar bowl and milk jug towards me, then slipped a teaspoon on the edge of my saucer. It didn't surprise me when he went on to say that he would be the one staying at home with Megan, his wife being the main breadwinner. I felt a small pang in my chest at the thought of all the changes Megan was going to have to adjust to, but I quickly chastised myself. Plenty of children thrived in the care of stay-at-home dads, and Francis seemed softer than his wife, gently considerate.

'What do you do, Mirella?' I asked as I stirred my tea.

'I'm a marketing executive with a large corporation,' she answered, her voice forthright and free of accent. It was easy to picture her standing beside a whiteboard and discussing methods of maximising brand exposure to a team of business associates. The idea bothered me, although I knew my feelings were irrational. I couldn't begin to define or unpick them, but I didn't feel entirely comfortable as she went on to explain her role and how much she enjoyed it. Francis watched me as his wife spoke and I looked between them, his short beard and round face contrasting with his wife's angular chin and sharp cheekbones.

In the next lull of conversation, Veronica asked me to tell the couple a bit about Megan. I was surprised by the composure in my voice as I told them about her routine, her likes and dislikes. Francis leaned forward, his hooded eyes shining with interest and amusement. It was clear that he loved children. Mirella nodded and smiled, though it was her husband who jumped in every now and again with pertinent questions. 'We just can't wait to meet her,' he told me, and then his brown eyes clouded with sympathy, 'though we realise it won't be easy for you. She's been with you for such a long time.' I nodded and forced a smile, wondering whether Veronica had revealed that my own application had been refused. I glanced at her but she didn't return my gaze.

'Endings are never easy,' I said, forcing a level tone. 'But I'll do my best to make sure it goes smoothly.'

Francis smiled kindly. 'Is there anything we can do to make it easier?'

Surprised by the question, I took a moment to consider. 'Keep in touch,' I said evenly. 'It would be a comfort to know she's happy and settled.'

Mirella's gaze flickered from me to her husband and then over to Veronica. Francis made another nervous, a-ha noise in his throat. My heart quickened. Had they already decided to make a clean break? The thought made my stomach swoop, but then Francis nodded forcefully. 'Of course, yes. That's understandable.'

Veronica tapped her palm on the table. 'Right,' she said, leaning forward and reaching below the table, her cheek almost touching the top. 'Here we are.' She handed a sheet of paper to each of us in turn. 'This is a draft timetable for the handover. Let me know what you think. It stretches across ten days, the first five in Rosie's house and then the last at yours.' She nodded towards Francis and Mirella. 'The idea is that you begin with just an hour or two on the first day, and gradually increase, but the plan is certainly not set in stone, so do let me know if you'd like to suggest changes.'

Mirella took charge then, making pencil notes on the sheet, angling it towards Veronica for her to consider. Watching them, it struck me that each of them had a positive, continuing role to play in Megan's life, whereas my own was coming to an end. Meeting Francis and Mirella had cemented the possibility of losing Megan into a reality. She would soon be leaving us, and there was now nothing I could do about it.

The best I could do was bow out gracefully, with as little upset to Megan as possible. Feeling like an outsider and strangely disconnected, my throat went dry, the muscles in my legs stiff and numb. For a fleeting, awful moment, I thought I might cry. Irritated with myself and feeling ridiculous, I stared out of the long window to the deserted, windswept street and, trying hard to compose myself, I hummed a little tune in my head.

The handover was a few weeks away and for the moment Megan was beyond their reach, happy and adored. I determined to make the most of every last minute we had together.

Chapter Thirty-Three

The knowledge that our time together was limited transformed the simplest events into tender moments filled with poignancy. Megan's first dreamy smile when she caught sight of me in the morning made my throat tighten and ache. When she ran to me and wrapped her arms around my neck, my eyes prickled with tears. After meeting Francis and Mirella, the mere sight of her induced such a mixture of emotions that part of me just wanted it over with, just wanted to put the pain in the past. The rest wanted to treasure every moment, stretch each one out and make them last.

Every morning I woke with a nagging sensation in my arms, as if hundreds of baby spiders were crawling through my veins. The impulse to go to Megan's bed and sweep her up to plant kisses all over her face was overwhelming. Instead, I made myself a mug of coffee and sat outside on my wicker chair, ignoring the cold. Children were expert at sensing subtle changes in mood or behaviour, so I knew it was important to keep to her usual routine.

I tried my best to keep my emotions in check, but at night I slept fitfully. Laying in the dark, my thoughts ran over themselves, worrying about what the future held for Megan. Would she carry a sense of loss with her for the rest of her life? I wondered. Wasn't that what often happened when children were adopted?

One morning towards the end of October, during half-term, all of the emotion of the last few weeks bubbled up, until I found I couldn't contain it.

It was a bright, cold day and we were all in the garden, the air around us tinged with the scent of burnt ashes and damp earth. When my mobile rang, I left Megan scooting between Emily and Jamie on her tricycle and went into the conservatory to answer it. It was Lesley Evans, the manager of Bright Heights Fostering Agency. Before Des left for the US I had rarely heard from Lesley, but in the absence of an allocated supervising social worker, there had been more contact between us in recent months. 'I'm sorry, Rosie,' she said, after a brief exchange of small talk. 'I know you're not going to be very happy about this but the local authority have asked that you surrender Megan's passport to us until the handover is complete.'

For a moment I couldn't respond. I was stunned. 'What do they think I'm going to do?' It was a daft question, but I couldn't believe their lack of trust. Did they really think I would abandon my life and run off into the sunset with a child who wasn't legally mine? Apparently Lesley had jumped to my defence and assured them that I wouldn't do such a thing, and she assured me that Veronica was simply following standard procedure, but I still felt hurt. 'Tuck it away with her other papers,' Lesley advised, at the end of the conversation. 'You'll need to pass it to the adopters when they come.' I was pleased that at least the agency had enough faith in me to leave the passport in my hands.

When Lesley ended the call I stood at the French doors and watched Megan stamping through the leaves. Jamie stood behind her, silhouetted by the low winter sun. Emily, crouching on her haunches nearby, scooped up handfuls of leaves and threw them in an arch over the toddler's head. Megan whirled around in the storm, eyes screwed up against the dust.

When Jamie joined in the game turned frantic, and soon the three of them were on their backs, making leaf angels on the grass and screeching with laughter. A minute or so later Jamie and Emily stood, still laughing, and pulled Megan to her feet. I watched as they crouched down and hugged her close, bits of crumpled leaves sticking to the backs of their clothes. Overcome with sadness, I put my face in my hands and stifled a sob.

Towards November, I began preparing Megan's life-story book. Hazel was preparing her own life-story book for Megan – focusing mainly on the story of her life before she came into care, including an honest account of the reasons her birth mum wasn't allowed to keep her – and she had asked me to prepare one from my own point of view.

Every foster carer was expected to keep an account of each child's stay with them, safeguarding the memories that would likely mean so much to them in later years, ones that other people learned naturally through the years from their birth parents. I knew from courses I had attended that adopted children tended to fill any gaps in the knowledge of their past with fantasies, so a story of their life in words and pictures, as well as being a comfort in later years, helped them to formulate an honest, realistic idea of how their early lives had passed.

Preparing Megan's life-story book was something I really wanted to do anyway. As the gatekeeper to her life story so far, it was the one last special thing I could do for her. Using ticket stubs, photographs with descriptive tags, souvenirs from special trips, birthday and Christmas cards, I chronicled each month of her life so far, including as much information as I could – developmental milestones, her favourite toys and childhood illnesses, an anecdote about the time she pooped in the bath.

My chest tightened as I went through her drawers, pulling out items from her earliest days. I tied little tags to each of them – her first sleep suit, her dummy, a tiny pair of socks – and wrapped them carefully in tissue paper before putting them in a memory box I'd ordered online.

Gripped by the urge to give her something personal, I also wrote her a letter. I had no way of knowing whether it would ever reach her – her new parents would navigate their own passage through the complex, choppy waters surrounding adoption – but if I was never to see her again, I wanted some way of communicating what I felt for her, so that one day, when she was old enough, she would know she had been loved as Peggy had prescribed; utterly and completely, no holds barred.

Dear Megan
Inside this box you will find some special items from the early weeks of your life. The first time we met you were wearing the tiny white sleep suit with small rabbits embroidered across the front, and when I brought you home from hospital you were wrapped in the crocheted pale yellow shawl. The little white rabbit was a gift from the midwives at Queen Charlotte's Hospital, who were so taken with you when you stayed in the special care baby unit, and the bonnet was knitted by your first social worker, Peggy.

I want you to know that we have treasured the time we were able to spend with you, Megan. It's been such a privilege to see your little character emerge and watch you grow. Please also know that you were loved from the moment I first held you in my arms.

It hurts to think of letting you go, but it helps to know that you are going to people who want you very much. I hope with all my heart that life is kind to you and that your new family love you as much as we do. We'll remember you always.

All our love
Rosie xx

I folded the letter up and put it in an envelope, my heart twisting as I tucked it into the bottom of the box.

Chapter Thirty-Four

In mid-November, a week before the handover was scheduled to start, I sat on the floor with Megan and drew a picture of our family. 'This is Rosie with Emily and Jamie,' I said, tapping the paper with my pen. 'And who do you think this little girl is?'

She frowned and then exclaimed 'Meggie!', patting her small hands on her chest.

'That's right. It's you.' We halted proceedings while she scribbled over the page using her felt-tip pens, and then I pulled out another sheet of paper. 'And here we have two very special people,' I said, sketching the figures of a man and woman. 'And they live in a beautiful house with a huge garden.'

When a move was planned for an older child, their social worker was usually the one to pass on the news, but with younger children, the business of breaking it to them often fell to the people they knew best and were closest to – their foster carers. I was pleased that Hazel had asked me to do it – since we spent every day together, it was easier for me to choose a moment when she was relaxed – but my stomach churned all the same.

Megan grabbed a felt-tip and lay flat on her tummy, her tongue poking through her lips with the effort of colouring in. 'Well done, Meggie, lovely colouring. Now, this nice man and lady don't have any children of their own,' I paused, licking my lips. I took a breath. My chest was beginning to hurt. 'And they would love it if you could be their little girl.'

Megan sat up and looked at me, frowning. I forced myself to look into her eyes. 'They'll play with you and love you and look after you,' I said, forcing a breezy, cheerful tone. 'Doesn't that sound nice?'

She thought about it and then shook her head. 'No, don't want to.' Those four words were the most favourite of combinations in her repertoire to date, so I knew I couldn't read anything into that particular response. Grabbing another pen, she stretched out on her tummy again and scribbled some large circles on the page.

I knew from moving other children onto adoption that Megan needed to feel sure that I approved of her leaving, if she was to attach fully to her new parents. I also knew that I had to drive the message home, even though it was likely to upset her. Veronica told me that children generally find it difficult to assimilate the concept that their old life is truly lost to them when they move to a new family. Convinced that their old carers are simply hiding somewhere out of reach, some spend weeks searching unfamiliar rooms, believing that if they look hard enough, they will find them.

If a child suspects there is a chance they can return to their old foster family when they move on to an adoptive placement, they remain loyal to their carer, effectively waiting in limbo. If I could have avoided a moment's pain for Megan then I would have done, but I couldn't bear to think of her feeling alone, unable to reach out to the people around her.

Having planted the seed in her mind, I got out her colouring books and changed the subject, but later that day and throughout the next I made a few references to Francis and Mirella in conversation, hoping that slowly, gently, the message would sink in. Megan barely reacted whenever I mentioned the possibility of living in a new family, listening with detached interest. It was as if we were playing a make-believe game she wasn't much interested in and I began to suspect that, at not quite two and a half, she was unlikely to understand the concept of moving on until it actually happened.

The next day it became clear that I was wrong about that, and when finally Megan reacted, I also realised that I wasn't at all ready for it myself. It had been one of those grisly days when she was out of sorts, so I didn't bring up the subject until bath time, when she was happier and relaxed. Picking up two of her plastic toy figures, I balanced them on the edge of the bath and bobbed them up and down. 'Look, Meggie, this is new Mummy and Daddy. They're very excited to meet you,' I said in a jovial tone.

'Don't want to!' she suddenly burst out. 'Me stay Mummy!' She began sobbing, tears rolling down her cheeks. Unprepared for such a reaction, I hurriedly grabbed a towel and lifted her out of the water. I sat on the edge of the bath and hugged her tight, the pain in my throat intensifying.

'It's all right, sweetie,' I said huskily, rocking her to and fro. She buried her head into my shoulder, her little body trembling in wet, shuddering sobs. It was horrible to see her so upset.

The nights that followed were restless and uncomfortable, full of disorientating dreams that left me feeling dazed when I woke in the morning. Sometimes, in fostering, the goodbyes were far too long and painful and I wished fervently that I could fast forward the days until the handover became a memory.

Each day I nudged Megan gently towards the idea of a new family, and every time I touched on the subject she stilled, watching me with a wide-eyed, doubtful expression. Ever since her outburst in the bath she had seemed wary, as if I might come out with some other strange and disturbing ideas.

'No!' she cried, on the eve of Francis and Mirella's first planned visit, when I told her that new Mummy and Daddy were soon coming for a cup of tea. Close to tears, she snatched her hand away from mine and stared at me resentfully, probably wondering why I kept pursuing an idea she had categorically dismissed days ago. Veronica had provided photos of Francis and Mirella and I gave them to Megan in the hope that she might feel closer to them when they finally met. I put them in her beloved Peppa Pig rucksack, but it wasn't long before they went missing. They turned up in the bin.

'Well, I thought it might be nice to make them some cakes to go with their tea. What do you think?'

'Yay!' she exclaimed, all objections forgotten. Megan loved making cakes; it was one of her most favourite pastimes. 'New Mummy like choc-choc?' she asked as she sat in front of me on the worktop and stirred the mixture.

'I'm sure she does,' I said with a smile, surprised by her sudden acceptance. For Megan's sake, there was nothing I wanted more than for the handover to go well, but I felt a niggle in my chest all the same. That we were part of her old life was a painful fact to accept, but slowly a future without Megan was taking shape in my mind.

Chapter Thirty-Five

On the last Monday of November 2013, paying no heed to Veronica's advice of taking things slowly, Mirella marched straight into the living room, sat next to Megan on the sofa and struck up a heavily one-sided conversation with her. Francis sat beside his wife, sweaty and nervous, interjecting whenever the opportunity arose, which wasn't often. Megan, who had been playing with her small dinosaurs, stared between them with a look of bewilderment. I knelt on the floor nearby, hoping to provide a reassuring presence, but after a few minutes she slipped off the sofa and buried her head in my skirt.

'Park now,' she said, getting up and tugging on my hand.

She nearly pulled me over. I put one hand to the floor to steady myself. 'Maybe later,' I said, glancing towards the couple. Mirella was wearing a fixed smile, but Francis looked crestfallen. I realised then how excited they must have been to meet their daughter for the first time, how long they must have spent dreaming of this moment. I felt a rush of sympathy for them.

'No,' Megan said, shaking her head and grabbing hold of my chin. She angled my face towards her and pressed her nose up against mine so that my nostrils flattened. 'Want park now.'

'I know,' I said in a loud stage whisper, my hand half-cupped over my mouth. 'But I've had an idea. Shall we try and guess what Mummy and Daddy like to drink? I think they might like worm juice with a sprinkling of ants. What do you think?'

Megan chuckled and looked at them. Mirella's expression softened into a genuine, doting smile but her husband still looked terrified. Megan's brow furrowed and she pouted. 'My think tea.'

Mirella clapped her hands together. 'You're right, Megan, clever girl.' Francis laughed in response, a little too loudly.

'Right, I'll make Mummy and Daddy some tea. How about you show them your Thomas the Tank engine set?'

'No, my do tea,' said Megan.

'Well, OK, you can help with the milk and sugar,' I conceded. The path of least resistance was the best way to go, I decided, for the first day of introductions. The sight of Megan in meltdown was something that was best served warm. Ten minutes later, Megan shuffled back in the room, the small tray of the cakes we'd made yesterday held out in front of her. 'Look new Mummy! Look Daddy!' she cried proudly. 'Cakes for you.'

'Oh, look at that!' Mirella exclaimed, glancing at her husband. 'Aren't they fantastic, Daddy?' Overcome, Francis didn't say anything. He nodded, his face suddenly flushed, his eyes misted over. Mirella patted his leg lovingly. She swallowed with difficulty, gathering herself. 'Who made these?' she asked, her eyes lingering on her husband. Picking up on the affection between them, and the warmth that had seemed absent a few weeks ago when I first met them in the café, I felt enormously relieved, comforted and touched. The knots of tension in my shoulders loosened.

'My did!' Megan exclaimed, in answer to Mirella's question. She patted her chest, looking terribly pleased with herself. I put their drinks on the mantelpiece and, leaving Megan to hand out the cakes, I slipped away to give them some space. Foster carers were supposed to slowly distance themselves during the ten-day handover period, gradually withdrawing to allow a relationship to develop between the child and their new parents.

In the kitchen I emptied one of the food cupboards and scrubbed the shelves, threw away some old tins and amalgamated all the odd packets of half-used pasta into one large jar. Suspended between roles, it was tricky to strike the right balance, but when Megan's chatter reached my ears, overlapped with laughter from her new parents, I thought perhaps it had been the right time to leave them alone. Reassured, I was surprised to find myself smiling at the sound.

'Poo!' Megan shouted, after about 20 minutes. 'I need a poo!'

In the living room, Mirella was staring at Megan with a panicked expression. Francis turned one way and then the other. 'Ooh, uh, OK,' he puffed, floundering. He came into his own the next afternoon, though, when Megan fell over and bumped her nose on the carpet. She started to cry and by force of habit I made a move towards her, but with Francis already on his feet, I stopped myself mid-step. My hands twitched at my side as he stooped over and swept her up. Slowly, I curled them into fists, making my arms rigid to stop myself from reaching out to her.

I was worried that his hesitancy might unnerve her, but sensing that he was needed seemed to give him confidence. He bobbed her around in his arms, hugging and rocking her. Mirella sat nearby, looking wistful and, though I couldn't be sure of it, a little left out. It felt weirdly unnatural to stand back and do nothing, and even more so when Megan's eyes met mine. Her brow furrowed in puzzlement 'Mummy!' she cried, reaching out to me.

Francis moved towards me. 'Rosie's here, it's all right,' he said soothingly, planting soft kisses in her hair.

I stroked her head. 'Daddy gives lovely hugs,' I said softly. Francis tilted his head and gave me a grateful smile.

Chapter Thirty-Six

Five days before the final handover my grief gathered momentum to the point where my stomach twisted itself in knots and my hands visibly shook. Determined to keep any upset away from Megan I swallowed down my feelings, forcing my mind to concentrate on the bigger picture – Mars One were recruiting astronauts on a one-way mission to another planet, for goodness sake – my worries were immaterial specks of dust in the vast universe. But suppressing my feelings didn't make them go away, they simply found another outlet, and three days before Megan was due to leave I woke up with a pounding in my head and a raging temperature.

The day passed in a blur of Lemsip, Olbas Oil and, after Mirella and Francis's visit, CBeebies on a loop. It was a relief to tuck Megan into bed that evening, but in the early hours she woke up crying. 'What is it, sweetie?' I asked, brushing her hair back from her forehead. She was clammy to touch, and when I picked her up, she was sick over my shoulder, all over the floor. 'It's all right,' I said soothingly, when she squealed and complained. 'We'll soon clean it up.'

I took her to the bathroom, dampened a flannel and washed her hands and face. Her pyjamas were damp so I pulled them off, dropped them on the floor and wrapped her up in a towel. She shivered. 'Tummy hurts,' she cried, her body sagging feverishly in my arms.

'I know, sweetie, I know. Let's pop you back in bed and get you some medicine.' In the bedroom I checked that her quilt was clean and dry then laid her down on the mattress. She flopped against the pillow and curled onto her side, whimpering.

'Urgh, stinks in here!' she squealed, but her eyes were already closing in sleep.

'Don't worry, I'll sort it out.' I ran downstairs to fetch the Calpol and a syringe. 'Meggie, darling,' I said a minute or so later as I tried to rouse her. Slipping one hand behind her head, I lifted her up and eased the tip of the syringe in her mouth. She moaned, her eyes flickering to narrow slits. 'Ready for medicine?' She gave a weak nod, swallowing obediently.

After tucking the duvet around her I grabbed handfuls of tissue from the bathroom and cleaned up the worst of the mess from the floor, then went downstairs and gathered the lemon-scented spray and a cloth. When the carpet was clean and I had changed my own pyjamas, I brushed her damp fringe out of her eyes and, hoping that rehearsing it might minimise some of the pain, I tried to imagine letting her go. She caught hold of my finger and sighed, allowing herself to drift into a deep, comforted sleep.

According to the handover schedule, Megan was to begin visiting Mirella and Francis in their own home the next morning, but she was too poorly for that. I rang Veronica and she agreed that Megan should stay indoors. 'I'll cancel contact for today,' she said in a surprisingly gentle tone. 'Keep her tucked up in the warm.'

Wrapped up in a duvet, we read *Hairy Maclary from Donaldson's Dairy* and the obligatory *Alfie and the Birthday Surprise*, and then watched *Bug's Life* until Megan stuck her thumb in her mouth and fell asleep. When she woke we launched straight into a surprisingly coherent, two-way conversation about dinosaurs at the seaside and by teatime, once Emily and Jamie got home, she had perked up enough to eat a bowl of tomato soup.

She was still a bit under the weather the next day, but since she wasn't running a fever, Veronica felt that contact with Francis and Mirella should go ahead. She fell asleep during the drive over to their house, and when I lifted her from her car seat she was a bit teary and disorientated. Sometimes, when she was woken early, she went into full-scale meltdown, thrashing herself around. Thankfully, the couple's beautiful house was breathtaking enough to distract her. As Francis and Mirella welcomed us into their large square hallway, Megan slipped her thumb in her mouth, her brow wrinkled in puzzlement.

Still quiet ten minutes later, she sat on my lap in the living room and stared around with intrigue, unaware that she was in the place she was likely to spend the rest of her childhood.

Foster carers are expected to mark the end of a placement with a party or special day out to encourage the child to view the move positively. With that in mind, there was no contact planned for the day before the final handover, Veronica setting the time aside for our family to say goodbye.

None of us were in the mood for a celebration, but my mum invited everyone over to her house anyway, decorating her small living room with banners and balloons. My sister-in-law Zoe ran up and threw her arms around me as soon as I walked in, and then my brothers Chris and Ben gave me a hug as well. My mum, overcompensating for our sombre moods, was theatrically jolly, laughing loudly and dishing out copious amounts of jelly and buttered buns. With all of us together, the atmosphere soon lightened. We took lots of photos for Megan's memory box, and my brothers, nieces and nephews gave her drawings and little keepsake gifts to take away with her.

Just before we left, Mum picked Megan up and hugged her fiercely. For all her bluster about keeping a stiff upper lip, I could tell she was battling to keep her emotions in check and I felt the tears gathering at the corners of my eyes as I watched them. It was hard to believe that by tomorrow Megan would be gone.

When Mum came over and passed Megan to me I couldn't speak. She patted me on the shoulder and kept her eyes focused somewhere else.

Chapter Thirty-Seven

On Wednesday 4 December 2013, almost two and a half years after I first held Megan in my arms, I strapped her into her car seat for the last time, and drove her towards her new life. We walked across the drive together, gravel crunching underfoot, Megan's small hand clasped in mine.

'Me ding-dong,' Megan insisted as we neared the house, her voice wobbly and tearful. Before leaving for school that morning, Emily and Jamie had said their goodbyes, and though they turned away to hide their tears, Megan had inevitably picked up on their mood. I still wasn't entirely certain that she knew what was about to happen, but it had been a disorientating week and she had been out of sorts for days, worn out and confused by the whole process.

'Yes, you can ring the bell,' I said soothingly. Feeling a little shaky, I took a deep breath to steady myself and then lifted Megan up onto my hip. At that moment Mirella opened the door, her husband hovering closely behind. My heart sank.

'No, no, no!' Megan screamed, kicking her legs and arching so far backwards that it was difficult to keep hold of her. 'Me do ding-dong!'

The couple's bright smiles faded instantly. Mirella instantly bustled into action, ready to take charge. 'What's wrong, Megan?' she asked, as if expecting a coherent explanation.

'Away!' Megan screeched, hand stretched out at arm's length. She pummelled the air. 'Go 'way!'

'Sorry,' I said, lowering the writhing child onto the pebbled drive. Part of what I was feeling, I realised, was disappointment. Secretly I had been willing Francis and Mirella to back out of the adoption, but here they were, ready to move on to a new, exciting phase of their lives. 'Megan was hoping to ring the bell.' Ashamed of the resentment I felt towards them, I used an apologetic tone.

'A-hhh,' they said in unison. Mirella backed away, made an impatient shooing motion in the direction of her husband and promptly closed the door. Megan, still absorbing the retreat, wasn't entirely sure whether to bestow us with a second chance. She carried on screaming for a few seconds longer before magnanimously deciding to forgive us.

'Ding-dong now,' she said frostily, reaching up to me.

The tension inside the house was palpable. 'May I get you some tea, Rosie?' Francis asked, hands poised in front of his stomach, fingertips touching. The thought of eating or drinking anything at that moment, even tea, made my stomach churn. 'Some cake perhaps?' he offered, when I refused, rolling his head one way and then the other. 'Anything at all?'

Mirella, in stark contrast to her husband's nervy attentiveness, was brisk and businesslike. 'Here's what we're going to do, Megan,' she said, drawing the child onto her lap. 'We're going to take your suitcase upstairs, spend a bit of time with Rosie, and then Mummy and Daddy will read you some books, OK?'

While Francis busied himself in the kitchen and Mirella took Megan upstairs, I went to the bathroom and splashed water on my face. Worried that I might be sick, I gripped hold of one of the twin enamel sinks and blew out some air. When the light-headed feeling passed I looked around the bathroom, taking in the gleaming stainless steel taps with matching silver accessories, the dark glass bottles in an immaculate line along the window sills, the wide-screen television sunken into the wall above an oval-shaped bath. It was difficult to imagine a child feeling at ease among the luxuries – splashing water over the fluffy bath rug, bath crayons and small foam letters of the alphabet across the marble tiles on the floor – but then perhaps it was just because I wasn't used to such neatness myself.

Downstairs, I sat with Megan in the playroom and set out her farm on the highly polished floor. It was one of the few toys that Mirella and Francis had agreed that she could bring with her – Mirella insisting that 'Francis and I much prefer wooden, traditional toys'.

I was pleased that at least Megan had something familiar to play with. Everything in the playroom smelled fresh and new, from the stack of new puzzles and toys in the corner, to the bookshelves and brightly coloured toy cabinets lining the walls. The house was beautiful, there was no doubt about that, but somehow soulless as well. I consoled myself with memories of my first home before Emily was born; the clean lines and scribble-free walls, everything in its place. Children had a way of rendering all of that unimportant, and I told myself that Megan would make a place for herself here, in time.

Megan sorted the animals into groups, one of her favourite tasks, while I set up the fences, the trees and the cobblestone barn. With everyone in their respective places, the misadventures began, Megan giggling as the pigs invaded the stable and a horse gatecrashed on the sheep. 'Get out my house!' Megan yelled, using small plastic bales of hay as missiles in an airborne attack. 'Boom, boom!'

'Play nicely now, Megan,' Mirella reminded her. Whether Megan heard or not I couldn't say, but she carried on regardless. After half an hour or so I caught Mirella's gaze and lifted my eyebrows. She nodded. 'I think it's time.'

With a pain in my throat, I told Megan it was time for me to go. She looked up and I opened my arms. As she had so many times before, she ran to me, snuggling herself into my chest. I badly wanted to tell her that I was sorry. I wanted to say that when I first picked her up and held her in my arms, from that very moment, I loved her. I wanted her to know that I wasn't good enough for her because she was so special but, oh my goodness, I was so very sad to let her go. Instead I pinched my lips together and closed my eyes.

I held her for what felt like a long time, although it was probably only ten or so seconds, stroking her back, relishing her warmth, and all the while knowing it was probably the last hug we would ever share. Somehow, Megan knew it too. She clasped her small hands around my neck, and there was none of the usual, impatient wriggling. 'Goodbye, sweetie,' I said huskily, planting a kiss on her hair and then pulling very gently away.

I wanted to say more, something cheerful and encouraging, but by then I was crying – I just couldn't stop myself. I grabbed my coat and bag and, without turning round, headed for the front door. Francis opened it, his expression full of compassion as I passed by. 'Where Mummy gone?' Megan cried out behind me, her screams making me question whether I had done the right thing in giving up my chance to keep her.

Tears trailed down my cheeks as I hurried to the car. I brushed them away with the back of my hand.

Chapter Thirty-Eight

Walking into the house was like turning up to a wake. It literally felt as if someone had died. My footsteps echoed as I moved from room to room, my eyes running over the row of rabbits along the shelf at the foot of Megan's little bed, the teddies that Mirella and Francis hadn't wanted to take scattered over the floor, the books I had read before tucking her into bed each night. And then my eyes took in the empty spaces. They were everywhere: the pillow, slightly indented where she had rested her head just a few short hours before, her *Bug's Life* beanbag and ballerina chair. I shivered, unable to believe she had finally, irretrievably, gone.

I had spent weeks pushing the nauseous ache away, but now, when I was finally free to give in to it, I felt nothing but a detached, fuzzy sadness. I tried to focus on the idea that I might see her again one day, but deep down I was convinced that Mirella and Francis wanted to draw a line under the past. I imagined instead a far-off day when

Megan might walk up the garden path as a grown woman, searching for the place she spent her earliest years.

After a quick cup of tea, I stripped all the beds, remade them, set the washing machine on a cycle, cleared out the already spotless kitchen cupboards and scrubbed the fridge, telling myself to look forward to the rare opportunity of putting my feet up at the end of the day. With no tea, bath and bedtime routine to stick to, I would be free to do whatever I wanted. Rather than cheering me, the thought made me feel empty and low.

It was a relief when Jamie came home from school, although even he barely raised a smile. There were so few times when Jamie was anything other than jokey and easy-going that it was unsettling to find him so morose. I forced a bright air around him and, still porous to suggestion, he brightened a little. Emily was too old to fall for that old trick though.

When she got in from work she met my cheery greeting with a wary look, as if I'd gone bonkers, and then offered to make dinner while I relaxed. I fixed my gaze on her; her cheeks were flushed, but otherwise she looked OK, if a little too contained. In the lead-up to Megan's handover she had tried so hard to be philosophical. 'It won't so bad, Mum, as long as we can still see her,' she had said more than a few times.

For a person who finds relaxation stressful, it was all I could do to sit on the sofa for a few minutes. What I felt like doing was laying down, pressing my face into one of the cushions and sobbing. I got through the moment by flicking through the *Radio Times* and repeatedly checking my phone. I kept hoping to hear from Mirella or Francis, to let me know that Megan was OK. Waiting around for a text was torturous, so I lit some candles and whiled away half an hour in the bath – an odd and strangely disorientating experience when it wasn't even 6 o'clock. Down in the kitchen, I stood beside Emily while she chopped some vegetables. 'You OK?'

She shrugged, not meeting my eye. 'Yep,' she said, but she was dragging a peeler along the carrots with fast, jabbing strokes. I took some crockery from the draining board and dried it with a tea towel, a previously unheard of activity in our house. As I put the plates and cups away in one of the cupboards, Emily peeled some mushrooms and washed small florets of broccoli under the tap. I could hear the water running, but at the sink, she suddenly stilled. After a pause she swung around, the colander still clutched in her hand. 'I miss her, Mum!' she said, tears rolling down her cheeks.

'I know. I do too.' Swinging the tea towel over my shoulder, I went over and pulled her into a hug. She sobbed on my shoulder. As I rubbed her back I glanced over at Jamie in the living room. He puffed out his cheeks and looked away, on the verge of tears himself.

If anyone had looked in on us as we ate our meal we would have made a sorry sight, each of us staring dumbly into our plates. I imagined Mirella and Francis wringing their hands and Megan, too upset to eat, refusing her tea. And then I pictured her wandering around all those new and strange rooms, pink rabbit clutched under her arm. When it came to thinking about her dropping off to sleep,

I shook my head abruptly. It was too uncomfortable to think about.

Veronica had assured me that her attachment to us would be swiftly eroded, as long as there was no contact between us. I hoped that was the case, though I found it difficult to believe that some memories wouldn't linger.

After washing up, we sat together and watched *Extras* back to back, each of Emily and Jamie's chuckles soothing the ache in my chest. We all went to bed around ten o'clock and, though exhausted, I lay awake, my thoughts still tormenting me. I kept worrying that Mirella and Francis might not love Megan as much as she needed them to. What if they resented her for waking in the night, something she was prone to do, or intruded on the time they usually spent as a couple? I told myself not to worry, and that they must be good people.

Their life, relationship, opinions and characters had been dissected and picked over by a number of different social workers. Friends of the couple had been interviewed, as well as all previous partners, work colleagues and siblings. I knew that only a fraction of those who expressed an interest in adopting a child actually went on to complete the assessment process, so there was no doubting Mirella and Francis's commitment. And if they loved Megan half as much as we did, she would be all right.

Anyway, it was none of my business. I kept telling myself that, and that worrying was futile, but it didn't stop me. I stared for a long time at the amber light creeping through the gap in the curtains from the street lamps outside. I turned onto my side and tried to empty my mind. For a minute or two, I cried.

I wasn't sure it was normal to hurt quite as much as I did. I knew other foster carers who seemed to manage moving children on easier than this. But then again, I had seen more of Megan in the last couple of years than anyone else, even my own children. Since contact with Christina had ended there had been barely an hour, in fact even a minute, when she hadn't been in my sight. Was it possible for a person to get that close to someone and not hurt when they were gone?

Added into the equation had been the potent suggestion that Megan might be able to stay with us. There had been so many twists and turns over the last two and a half years, so many opportunities raised and then blighted.

With no inkling that the biggest twist in Megan's story lay in the future, not the past, I prayed hard it wouldn't be long before she forgot us.

Chapter Thirty-Nine

When I woke the next morning, the ache in my throat reminded me instantly that Megan was gone. All of yesterday's drama had numbed some of the upset, but this morning her loss hit me with full force. My chest felt sore on the inside, almost as if sand were flowing through my lungs instead of air.

As the winter sun crept in through the gap in the curtains, I wondered whether Megan had already woken and how she felt when she opened her eyes in an unfamiliar place. Had she called out for me, I wondered. Did her stomach lurch when she realised I was gone? I hoped not.

The house felt uncomfortably quiet when Emily and Jamie left that morning. I watched at the window as they crossed the road and rounded the bend towards the crossroads, keeping my eyes fixed at the point where they were lost from sight. Opposite stood a row of small houses and a bit further along, a low fence and then a gap, where a footpath led to an open stretch of grass. At the edge of my vision I caught a glimpse of the small play park Megan had loved so much.

Everything – the swings, the slide and see-saw – looked too quiet, too uncomfortably calm. Inside my head it felt as if so much was different, yet there it all was, solid and unchanged. Every now and again I was seized by panic, as if I'd been distracted by something in the supermarket and while my back was turned, Megan had vanished. I kept telling myself that she was safe, but somehow the message wouldn't seep through to my brain.

Deciding that fresh air and exercise might help me to shake off some of the anxiety, I took myself off for a walk. Without Megan beside me though, and no destination in mind, I stalled early, just outside my own gate. Swaying on my feet, I turned one way and the other. The park was out of the question – the band around my chest tightened at the mere thought of it, and I hadn't the heart to walk along the river either, another place Megan had adored.

After a few false starts I headed towards the shops, feeling a little more positive with a direction in mind. Everywhere I went, though, the empty space at my side shadowed me. A constant reminder of her absence, it became all the more noticeable as the streets widened and dipped towards town – no broad smiles from strangers as they passed by, no one stopping to say hello.

I paused outside one of the gift shops and was about to go in when I spotted one of my neighbours inside, talking to an elderly man with silver hair behind the counter. Beryl had fostered children decades earlier, back in the days when placements were advertised in local newspapers, and she and her husband Ted still shared a passion for it. They often bought the children I looked after a little something for Christmas and both had had a soft spot for Megan.

I knew Beryl was likely to ask how the handover had gone so I hesitated on the pavement. Perhaps sensing my presence, she glanced up, her eyes widening in recognition when they settled on me. She must have read the upset in my face, because her own expression faltered and her lips bunched up, her eyes wrinkled and sad. I gave her a wan smile and turned quickly away, grateful for the patches of condensation on the glass.

Seeking sanctuary in chores, I went home and hoovered downstairs. Afterwards, I cleaned out the cupboard under the sink, the last place in the whole house that hadn't been subjected to a blitzing, and then climbed into the loft and got the Christmas boxes down. Emily would want to hang the decorations, but I knew she wouldn't mind me doing the boring stuff. It was while I was constructing the artificial tree and trying hard to keep my mind away from Megan that another thought took hold – the idea that we should move house. I decided to look online and see what was available in our price range. Worried about taking on a mortgage alone, I had been procrastinating about it for over a year, but now, with a bit of time on my hands and interest rates still at a record low, I convinced myself it was high time I took decisive action.

By half past ten, just as I had sat down and logged on to one of those property websites, the doorbell rang. On high alert, my heart jumped into my throat. As soon as I opened the door, my mother marched in and drew me into a hug. She smelled of Blue Grass perfume and Tic Tacs. 'How come everyone else manages this so much better than me?' I asked later, as she fished a neglected teapot out of one of my immaculately clean cupboards.

She put the pot down and folded her arms. After a long time she said, 'Maybe some are just better at hiding it than you. You've always worn your heart on your sleeve.'

I nodded. 'I loved her so much, Mum.'

She took my hand in hers and squeezed it. 'I know you did. And all that love isn't lost. It'll stay in her heart. When she's older she's going to want to know who put it there, you mark my words. Though I'll be in my box by then, I shouldn't wonder.'

I groaned and pulled my hand away to dab my eyes with a tissue. 'I told you this would happen. I warned you,' Mum said. She sounded annoyed, but her face was full of compassion. 'Her first two and a half years were very happy. We can't ask for more than that.'

When I called Peggy later that day she put me in my place. 'So you think you're indispensable, do you? You think no one else can provide what you did for her. Stop magnifying your own importance and get on with your life,' she said, in that head-nodding, definite tone of hers that put me in mind of Nigel Farage. I found her words strangely comforting.

Helen brought fish and chips over that night. 'Oh God, here we go,' she groaned when she caught sight of me. 'I suppose she's going to be insufferable all evening,' I heard her say in the kitchen as she helped Emily put the food on the plates. The two of them occasionally met up for meals or a drink without me and had their own little friendship going on. The ache inside me lifted at the sound of their banter.

'Why don't you do something else less stressful?' Helen said, as we sat on the sofa eating dinner from trays on our laps. I'd actually been thinking along the same lines myself.

'Don't say that, Helen!' Emily cried. 'We love fostering.'

'But what else?' I said. 'Fostering is all I've ever wanted to do.'

Helen thought for a moment. 'They're looking for help at the local garden centre. Even you can't get attached to rocks.'

I laughed, spluttering on my mouthful. In that moment, the pain in my chest faded again. It returned with a vengeance moments later, but the memory of it was a comforting reminder that there was a way past the sad, empty ache.

Emily and Jamie bellowed as Helen came up with increasingly ludicrous suggestions for making a living. It was so good to see them laugh.

After dinner we watched *Skyfall*, but, worn out with all the emotion of the last few weeks, I fell asleep halfway through. 'Well, thanks for a lovely evening,' Helen said sardonically, as the credits rolled. I blinked myself awake, apologising. I loved friends I could fall asleep in front of. 'It's like the Night of the Living Dead round here,' she moaned as she pulled on her coat. But she gave me an extra-tight hug on the way out.

Soon after Helen left I got the news I had been waiting for – a text from Mirella saying that Megan was doing fine. It was such a comfort to know that she was coping well, and I felt as if a heavy weight had been lifted from my shoulders.

Chapter Forty

It was difficult to imagine anyone else staying in Megan's room, but about two weeks after she left, just a week before Christmas, I accepted a new placement – Josh, a 12-year-old boy with mild learning difficulties. Since the age of five Josh had lived with his maternal grandmother, but after a fall and a brief stay in hospital, she had been diagnosed with dementia. Her condition was advanced, enough for her to be admitted straight into a nursing home, and social workers believed that both she and Josh had remained silent about the symptoms for a long time, for fear of being separated.

Josh was a vulnerable character, but gentle and calm. Not surprisingly, he was heartbroken to leave his grandmother and my heart went out to him when he arrived at our door, head down, hands shoved deep inside his pockets. As soon as I set eyes on him I felt a motherly longing to chase away his sadness.

He shadowed me for the first few days, his brown eyes darkened with grief. In the evenings, when we sat down to watch television, he stared into space with an uncertain, slightly puzzled frown. I wasn't certain that he totally understood his grandmother's illness, but I think he knew he was slowly losing her, a pain that was difficult enough for someone three times his age to deal with.

Life had afforded him some cruel blows – after leaving him with his grandmother, his mother left the country and had never bothered to keep in touch – but Josh never complained about anything. After making a casual remark about liking chocolate spread, I bought him a jar from the corner shop to put on his toast. You would have thought I'd handed him a ticket to travel the world. The tiniest kindnesses pleased him.

It was the same on Christmas Day. The whole extended family met up for dinner at my brother Chris's house and, as usual, all of them were thoughtful enough to bring a gift for Josh. When my brother was sharing out the presents, Josh retreated into the shadows of the room, as if he expected to be excluded. He got quite teary when he saw that there was a pile of gifts especially for him.

Jamie's good-humoured teasing slowly made an impact and helped bring Josh out of himself, and he was greatly cheered when his social worker, a young, newly qualified Australian, organised twice-weekly contact with his grandmother at the nursing home. On Tuesdays and Thursdays I waited for him in the relatives' room while he spent some time with her, and in some ways it was a luxury to have a break enforced on me.

The television in the day room was always on, but set to a low volume. On my first visit, some of the residents watched me curiously as I threaded a path around the low coffee tables and armchairs, others dozed. Sitting in a high wing-backed chair by the window, I spent the time reading, and the hour flew by.

Some of the mothers at our local toddler group ran an unofficial book club, and one of the books given to me was *Madeleine* by Kate McCann. It was an uncharacteristic read for me – I usually prefer novels – but I was quickly drawn into the story. With each passing chapter I found myself hoping desperately for a happy resolution, although of course I knew there wasn't one. When I reached the end of the book, I felt almost ashamed for spending so much time feeling sad about Megan.

There were people in the world who had suffered the worst kind of loss, and yet the little girl we loved was safe and warm and well cared for. I missed Megan terribly, we all did, but I had chosen to foster her, knowing that there would inevitably be an ending. And in the end I had chosen, albeit reluctantly, to let her go without a fight. Adoption was the happiest ending I could possibly have hoped for.

Gradually a rhythm returned to the days. I introduced a strict schedule for school hours, when the house was quiet and I noticed Megan's absence most keenly. In the mornings I cleared away the breakfast things, put a wash on and wrote up my daily fostering diary, and in the afternoon I whizzed around the house, pulling sheets from the beds, putting clothes away and tidying up. The rituals worked their magic, quelling any anxiety I might feel for Megan.

Strictly speaking, as I had been fostering Megan for so long, I was entitled to one last contact with her, six weeks after the handover, but after that, any future contact was entirely at Mirella and Francis's discretion. Apart from that one text, I hadn't heard anything from either of them, and I felt a vague sense of disquiet at the silence.

My uneasiness grew in early January, when I received a call from Veronica. She told me, with surprising tenderness, that the Howards had received our Christmas card, but would prefer it if we didn't send birthday and Christmas cards to Megan in the future. They felt that it was unsettling for her to be reminded of her past.

I could understand their reasoning, but I wondered why they couldn't have just kept the cards tucked away in a box at the bottom of their wardrobe. Veronica said that I should continue to send the cards, but address them to her. 'It's not unusual for this to happen,' the social worker explained in a regretful tone. 'Adopters don't like constant reminders of the past. It's important that you still send them though, Rosie. I'll keep a box with Megan's file and store them for her here.'

I longed to see that Megan was settled in her new family, but if the Howards couldn't bear to receive cards from me, I felt there was little chance they could manage face-to-face meetings. I didn't want to make any demands.

Francis and Mirella were going through a major adjustment in their life and I was sure that they had enough to cope with, without worrying about me.

I hoped to hear more from them as the weeks went by, but a few days after Veronica's call, I heard from Hazel. She had paid the Howards a planned, final visit before closing the file her end, and she told me that as soon as Megan saw her she shrieked with delight and ran to fetch her coat. Hazel gently explained that she was there to make sure everything was OK, not to take Megan back to me, but Megan had sobbed and cried, pleading with Hazel to take her home.

Part of me was grateful for Hazel's honesty, and she reassured me that Francis and Mirella were able to comfort Megan before she left, but her words still broke my heart. Worse still, I suspected that the incident might lead Mirella and Francis to think that future contact with our family might be a little too painful for everyone.

Ten weeks after Megan left us, we finally moved into a home of our own.

Planning the move and packing up our belongings had taken weeks, but it was a distraction I had been grateful for. I had been so busy that there'd been moments in the day when my worries subsided and I forgot all about Megan. My chest would stop aching, but then, as I pulled out the old junk buried at the back of a cupboard, or cleaned the gap between the sofa and the wall, I'd come across a long-forgotten toy or one of Megan's socks, and another memory would grip hold of my heart.

My throat ached as I locked the front door of the home we had rented for almost a decade for one final time. In some ways it felt as if we were leaving Megan behind. My arms still ached to hold her.

Chapter Forty-One

'I really shouldn't be telling you this,' Veronica said, her voice lowered conspiratorially. 'But I felt you had a right to know.'

It was February 2014 and we had been living in our new house for just over a week. I still hadn't fully unpacked and the telephone was resting on an upside-down tea chest. I grabbed the cradle and pressed the base against my stomach, walking along the hall until the cord protested at full stretch. 'What? Is Megan OK?' I asked. There was a pause. My heartbeat accelerated. 'Veronica?'

'She's OK, yes. But the placement has disrupted.'

A tingle the size of an electric shock ran through me. 'Oh no!' My voice wobbled. 'Poor Megan.'

'It's dreadful, truly dreadful.' I had come to associate Veronica with cold practicality, so I was surprised to hear her own voice shaking with emotion. 'It's the one situation we really never want to deal with.'

'No,' was all I could say. 'No.' My head was spinning.

There was another pause, and then Veronica said, in a voice not quite as precise as usual, 'I can only imagine what you must be thinking.'

'Believe me, I take no delight in being right about something like this.' If I'm honest, though, I did feel a flicker of righteous vindication. But then I thought about Megan, knowing that, right at that moment, she was probably hurting, and there was nothing I could do to make it better. 'What happened?'

Veronica heaved a heavy sigh. 'Reading between the lines, and this is just between you and I, Francis is besotted with Megan, but Mirella is struggling to adjust to motherhood. It's something we see from time to time; one partner failing to bond and the other one resenting the lost attention. It's not a good position to be in, for any of them.'

'So where is Megan now?'

'Still with the Howards. We've been working with them to see if we can help them through with extra support, but there really is no way back from where they are, I'm afraid.'

'She's still there? Will she be OK? Shouldn't we go and get her right now?' I could hardly bear to think about how frightened she must be if Mirella and Francis weren't coping well. I felt a band close tight around my throat at the thought.

'No, no. It's not ideal, but she's safe. She's coming back into care in the next few days.'

I ran my hands through my hair. I wanted to get into my car and drive straight over there to pick her up. 'Well, she can come today as far as I'm concerned. It won't take long to get things ready.'

'Ah, well, it's, um, it's not as straightforward as that,' Veronica said, and something in her tone sent my pulse racing again. 'The plan is for her to go to one of our in-house carers.'

'What?' I stopped mid-step. I couldn't believe what I was hearing. 'That's madness! How can you do that to her? She'll be so confused.'

'I don't disagree with you. I've had words with the access to resources team, but I have no authority over them.'

Suddenly it all made sense. Since I fostered through a private agency, the local authority would save money by using one of their own carers. 'So we're talking about saving money, rather than a child's emotional welfare.'

'Rosie, I'm putting my neck on the line just by giving you this information. What you do with it from here on in is down to you. I just felt it was my duty to tell you. Strictly speaking, this has nothing to do with you.'

I felt a surge of gratitude towards Veronica, but I didn't tell her so. My mind was already swelling with myriad thoughts. 'I'll waive my allowances,' I suddenly burst out, certain I'd found an instant solution. 'If it's all about the money, the local authority can pay the agency fee, but keep mine. That way it won't cost them any extra to use me.'

'It's worth suggesting,' Veronica said, with a surprising degree of tenderness. 'But it's unprecedented. I'm not sure they'd go along with that. Whatever action you decide to take, Rosie, please don't bring my name into it.'

Chapter Forty-Two

I slowly replaced the receiver in its cradle and sank down on the bottom tread of the stairs, the phone resting on my lap. I knew the local authority had a responsibility to save money and direct resources where they were most needed, but surely there had to be some leeway, when the welfare of the child was at risk?

I rested my head against the newel post, the cold surface of the wood honing my thoughts to a single, narrow objective – I had to try and get Megan back, There was no way I could stand aside while she was bounced around the system, possibly moving from carer to carer until another place of permanency was secured. I couldn't give up on her, at least not without a fight. With the absolute and certain knowledge that it was the right thing to do, a feeling of calm swelled inside me.

It was difficult to know what to do first though. If I approached the local authority and challenged their decision they would demand to know how I came by the knowledge of the disruption, before it had even officially happened. There was no way I was going to compromise Veronica's position, not after she'd taken a risk in contacting me. I didn't want to land her in any trouble.

I tapped the receiver gently on my forehead, racking my brains for a solution. And after a few minutes all of the options I thought of were reduced to one – I was going to have to contact Mirella or Francis. I was in little doubt that they were probably going through one of the lowest, most awful times in their lives and I felt bad for intruding on them. But I also needed to take action as soon as I possibly could, if I wanted to interrupt social services' heavy, bureaucratic wheels.

I ran to the kitchen, where breakfast bowls, plates with crusts of toast and cereal packets still littered the worktops, and grabbed my mobile. Quickly, I typed out a bland text:

Hi Mirella, how are things? I hope you're OK,
Rosie x

When I pressed 'SEND' I was gripped by a sudden feeling of connectedness with Megan. I closed my fingers around the handset, trying to keep hold of the feeling. My stomach tensed with fresh, steely resolve and, with a rush of energy that had been absent for weeks, I searched for a notepad and pen then sat at the computer and switched it on.

It occurred to me then that my first port of call should be my fostering agency, Bright Heights. I tried their number but the line was engaged so I left a message asking for someone to call me back. I still had no supervising social worker, although Lesley Evans, the agency manager, had assured me she was available anytime, if ever I needed advice or support.

I had heard that The Fostering Network were a good source of information for carers, so I scanned their website and then dialled the advice and mediation number. The adviser, a woman with a mature, slightly quivery voice, listened patiently as I outlined the situation, interjecting occasionally with questions of her own. When I'd finished speaking she told me that, as far as she knew, the local authority were under no obligation to place Megan back with me, but she felt strongly that they had a moral duty to do so. She advised me to contact Adoption UK to check my legal position, and asked that I let her know the outcome.

I was beginning to feel much more positive. There seemed to be a little more hope, although I was afraid to indulge the idea in case I was wrong.

The legal adviser at Adoption UK was exceptionally helpful. While he wasn't sure whether a break in my care stripped me of my right to make a direct application to adopt Megan through the family court, he echoed the view of the adviser at The Fostering Network, saying that the local authority had a duty to act in the best interests of the child. 'In my opinion,' he said, 'that means returning the little girl to people who love her. Tell the local authority that you've sought legal advice and see what they say,' he added, and then, amazingly, he offered to accompany me if I could get them to agree to a face-to-face meeting. I thanked him, noted down the contact details of solicitors with specialist knowledge of child-custody issues and ended the call.

I managed to speak to one of the solicitors immediately afterwards, and was surprised to hear that she was already representing numerous other foster carers, some of whom had been turned down as adopters by their respective local authorities, and others who were seeking contact orders to give them the legal right to stay in touch with children who had moved on to adoptive placements. 'If a child has been in your care for a year or more you have a right to make an Annex A application to the court,' she told me, 'but I believe you lose that right if there's a break in that care. I'm not one hundred per cent sure on that, but I'll find out and get back to you.'

At the end of our conversation, she told me that she thought it was lovely that I cared so much about Megan and offered to represent me for free on a pro bono basis. 'It would be my pleasure,' she said, 'for you and for Megan.' Touched and very grateful, I couldn't disguise the wobble in my voice as I said goodbye.

As soon as I ended the call my phone rang. I recognised Mirella's number on the display and my heart began to race.

'Rosie,' she said, with no trace of her usual assuredness. Her voice was flat and she sounded very low. 'I'm afraid things haven't gone well at all.' She went on to tell me that Megan hadn't settled as they'd hoped and then, unexpectedly, her sister had fallen ill. 'It's just too much to cope with at the moment,' she sobbed, but then she sniffed, suddenly quietening. 'But surely you know all of this, if she's coming back to you?'

Taken by surprise, I didn't say anything. In the background, I could hear the sound of Francis's voice. My stomach tightened with the thought that Megan was probably right there, beside him. And then I heard her little voice. Just briefly. Only one or two words, but the effect was potent. My legs turned to jelly. My chest filled with fresh resolve.

'She – she is coming back to you – isn't she?' Mirella asked querulously. 'We asked specifically and –'

'I'm about to call the local authority,' I said evasively. In reality, Mirella had no right to dictate what happened to Megan next, any more than I did. She was crying hard by then, and after a hasty goodbye she rang off.

Chapter Forty-Three

I couldn't get hold of Hazel. I left a message, but when school-run time came round, I still hadn't heard anything back from her or from Lesley at Bright Heights. I longed to talk to Emily about it when she got home, but I knew that she was still missing Megan. If she caught a whiff of what was going on she'd be on tenterhooks all evening like I was. I didn't want to get her hopes up until I knew whether we were in with a fighting chance of keeping her.

The evening dragged. I couldn't wait for morning to come, and all I could think about as I tried to get to sleep that night was how lost Megan must be feeling. Even if Francis and Mirella were managing to go through the motions of caring for her, when it came to emotions, children were fiercely astute.

Hazel rang back around noon the following day. I had spent the morning cobbling a plan together and when I heard her voice I was ready to launch into a speech about having heard from Mirella that the adoption wasn't going ahead. In the event, she didn't even ask how I knew. But what *she* told me really took the wind out of my sails. 'When was this?' I asked, leaning back in my computer chair. I was reeling. It seemed that Hazel had contacted Bright Heights Fostering Agency to tell them the news about Megan, but staff there had informed her that I no longer had a vacancy.

'As soon as I heard about a possible disruption, so, what? About two weeks ago, I'd say. I'm surprised they didn't tell you.'

I didn't say anything for a second or so; I was livid. 'I've only got one child here at the moment. I can make room for Megan.'

'I thought you only had one spare room?'

'I do, but I can easily convert the dining room into a bedroom for me.'

'Really? You'd do that?' Hazel made a humming noise, as if she was considering it. 'I'm not sure the rules would allow it.'

'I've done it before and they were fine with it.' It was true. Years earlier I had been encouraged to make space for siblings, Taylor and Reece, since they were too old to share the same room, although that had been for a different local authority. Across the country, the rules and procedures varied. I had heard of carers dividing double bedrooms into two, sometimes even three tiny sleeping pods using MDF partitions, to accommodate looked-after children. To me that seemed unfair, but social service departments were often willing to stretch the rules, when it suited them.

'Hmmm, well, there's another strategy meeting this afternoon with the adoption team. I'll raise it with them. I want Megan back with you, believe me. I've said my piece in no uncertain terms, and so have others in the fostering team. The problem is our access to resources team. They won't approve the extra expense of using an agency carer when we have several of our own in-house carers waiting for a placement.'

Hazel sounded genuine in her regret, but was taken aback when I said I would forgo my allowances if Megan was allowed to return to me. 'I don't know how that would work,' she said. 'I've never heard of that before.'

Disappointment washed over me. I felt thoroughly let down by Bright Heights and assailed by a feeling of betrayal. 'Don't feel too disheartened, Rosie. I'll press the point at the meeting this afternoon. Don't give up hope.'

From the desk drawer I took out my notebook and scanned the notes I had made during my consultation with the legal adviser from Adoption UK. I remembered what Peggy had said about Hazel bending with the wind. I liked her as a person, but I wasn't confident enough in her tenacity to leave it to her. It was time to bring out the big guns. 'With all due respect, Hazel, I don't want to rely on hope. Can I speak to the manager of Children's Services, please?'

Hazel took a noisy breath. 'Andrew Cohen? That might not be easy. His schedule is usually pretty tight.'

Off the cuff, and without thinking about it long enough to waver, I summoned a tone Peggy might have been proud of, one that wasn't going to take no for an answer. 'I need to let him know that I'm intending to seek legal advice.' I went on to tell Hazel that advisers from The Fostering Network and Adoption UK were both of the opinion that social services arguably had a moral duty to place Megan with people who loved her, rather than any legal obligation.

A few seconds of silence followed. I sensed some confusion. Hazel certainly hadn't been expecting that sort of riposte. But her reaction took me completely by surprise. Instead of being put out by my insistence of going over her head, she sounded rather thrilled. 'I see,' she said, in a slightly breathless tone. 'In that case I'd better try and put you through straight away.'

Less than two minutes later I heard another voice on the line, this one deep and commanding. It was Andrew Cohen, the big boss. My insides knotted up and I suddenly felt completely out of depth. I started talking before a crisis of confidence set in. I began with a potted summary of our time with Megan, telling him about our application to adopt her, Veronica's initial agreement and the subsequent rejection.

'She was with you for two years, you say?'

'Nearly two and a half.'

'On what grounds were you refused?' he asked, his matter-of-fact tone giving nothing away.

Quickly, I told him about Megan's birth mother being aware of our whereabouts and the adoption team's risk assessment. I went on to explain about the current circumstances and that we had since moved home, and ended by telling him that we were desperate to offer Megan the stability she so badly needed.

'So what's the problem, then?' There was a note of impatience in his tone, but if I was to put money on the reason for it I would have said he was exasperated with the staff in his own department, if anything. I told him about the access to resources team and their decision to use in-house carers. He mumbled something about that being the usual policy, and my heart sank, but he followed up by thanking me for bringing the issue to his attention.

I wasn't sure what to think when he ended the call, but as soon as I put the telephone down I opened a document on the computer and reiterated my intention to seek legal advice. I printed the letter immediately and hand delivered it to the local authority municipal buildings that afternoon.

Josh stayed behind after school that afternoon for remedial maths, and Emily and Jamie were out with their dad. When the phone rang at just after 5 p.m., I was standing at the window in the living room, watching out for their return. Gary's car pulled into sight just as I registered Mr Cohen's voice, headlights sweeping across the grass verge outside.

I hadn't expected to hear back from social services so soon, and especially not from someone in his senior position. I knew that an emergency strategy meeting had taken place, but the bureaucratic wheels usually turned slowly, and it often took a while for information to filter through to foster carers. 'I have news, Rosie,' he said, but his tone was unreadable.

I walked slowly to the hall as I listened, my mobile clamped tightly to my ear.

'I see. Yes. Thank you very much for letting me know.'

I ended the call, slipped my phone onto the lowest stair and yanked the door open. Emily and Jamie quickened their step towards the house. 'What is it, Mum?' Emily said, staring at me with concern.

I cupped my hands over my cheeks and beamed at them. 'You're not going to believe it!'

Chapter Forty-Four

I set off early on the following Monday morning, hardly able to contain my excitement. The air was sharp and raw and my car heater wasn't working but there was so much adrenaline surging through my veins that I hardly noticed the cold. Traffic was heavy and I tapped feverishly on the steering wheel as my Fiat rolled along, as if the effort might make the journey shorter.

My thoughts tumbled over themselves, wondering how Megan would react when she saw me. Would she run to me? Or had the last few months dulled her memory, transforming me into no more than a stranger? The picture of her that I held in my head was already beginning to go fuzzy at the edges. How much more quickly did the past fade for a child?

At last the road branched left and swelled outwards so that the children's centre came into view. My heart quickened. The car park was almost empty but I was a little early so I drove on, parking in a side road about 150 yards away. Walking back, I started to wonder whether I too might feel disconnected from her, and whether our short separation had altered the bond between us.

When I reached the contact centre I scanned the windows hoping to catch a glimpse of her, but there was no sign. I pressed the intercom fixed to the wall beside the main door and, as I waited, a sudden elation washed over me. The receptionist asked me to sign in and my hands shook as I clutched the pen.

She gestured for me to take a seat in the large rectangular waiting area with several closed doors leading off to various playrooms and offices. I sat down, but only for half a second. I couldn't keep still. I paced the tiled floor instead, my gaze flitting from the water cooler to the noticeboards and over each of the closed doors. My heart raced with excitement, rising until it was almost too much to bear.

A flash of movement on the far side of the lobby caught my attention. At the sound of footsteps, I spun around. And there she was – Megan – standing in one of the doorways, holding Hazel's hand.

My heart jolted.

It was tempting to run over, pick her up and swing her high in the air, but I held myself back, crouching down instead. 'Megan, darling,' I said, tears misting my eyes. I couldn't help myself. It was so wonderful to see her.

She seemed hesitant. 'Mummy?' she asked, looking thoroughly confused. Hazel must have told her where she was going, surely? But then it occurred to me that if Hazel had said she was taking her to see Mummy, it wouldn't have been at all clear which one they were talking about. The thought made my stomach clench. 'Sweetie, it's Rosie,' I said, holding out my arms.

And then she ran to me, tears overflowing and rolling down her cheeks. Pulling her to me, I sat back on the floor and swept her onto my lap, stroking her wet cheeks with my forefinger. 'There, it's alright. Don't cry, honey,' I crooned, but I was in tears as well. I could hardly believe she was back in my arms. The feeling of joy was indescribable.

It was only a few moments later that the differences struck me. She was taller, definitely, but bonier too, the angles of her ribs jutting out so that I could feel them as I cuddled her to me. I brushed my hand over my eyes and gently eased her away, holding her at arm's length so that I could look at her.

'Where been?' she asked, searching my face with red, teary eyes. She sounded angry then, resentful.

I stared at her, lost for words. How on earth could I put what had happened to her into words that someone who was not quite three would understand? Hazel saw me floundering and crouched down next to her. 'Do you remember what I told you, Megan? About the adults who care about you wanting to find the best place for you to live? Well, adults sometimes make mistakes. We've realised that, for now, the best place for you to stay is with Rosie. Is that OK?'

Megan threw her arms around me in answer, closing them tightly around the back of my neck. My heart soared. For the first time in weeks, the heavy stone weight in my chest lifted.

Chapter Forty-Five

Megan was beside herself when I strapped her into the car. 'Mine seat!' she kept shouting, running her small hands over the dog-eared fabric as if it were a luxurious silk. 'Mine seat back!'

I kept up a steady stream of chatter on the way home, telling her all about our new house in the hope that she wouldn't be too confused when we got there. So much had changed in her little life, but things had moved on for us as well. I worried that it might be all a bit too much for her.

'Nuther house?'

'Yes, a lovely new house. Emily and Jamie are there. And another boy called Josh.'

'Don't want nuther house. Want old house.'

'You'll like it there, sweetie. It's nice.'

'Nuther house?' she kept repeating, as if she was trying to get used to the idea but couldn't quite bring herself to. My heart ached for her. After all the changes she'd experienced, she craved familiarity, something steady to hold on to.

A few roads from home I pulled over and sent my mum a text to say we were two minutes away. The plan was for Emily, Jamie, Josh and Mum to wait outside for us to arrive, so that Megan would see some friendly faces before encountering the unfamiliar house.

I tried to breathe normally, but I was so excited for Megan to see the others that my lungs refused to play along with my efforts. A tree surgeon's van was parked in front of our small drive, so I pulled up against the kerb on the other side of the road and quickly pulled the keys from the ignition.

My hands shook as I lifted Megan from the car. 'Where going?' she cried, becoming anxious. Her bottom lip began to tremble and she tightened her grip on my shoulders.

'We're going home to Rosie's new house. Do you remember I told you we moved to a different place?'

But she clearly believed it was all a ruse to drop her off with someone else. She threw herself backwards and tried to scramble away from me, back to the car. It was a struggle to keep hold of her.

'Hey, hey, hey, what's all the noise?' I heard my mum call out. Megan froze mid-tussle, then looked at me.

'N-anny?'

I smiled. 'Yes, it's Nanny!' It had only been a few months, but I was surprised that she was able to recognise my mother by the sound of her voice alone. She wriggled to get down and ran towards the sound. Emily and Jamie came into sight first, around the side of the green van.

'Megan!' Emily shouted, holding out her arms. Within seconds Emily and Jamie had enfolded her into a hug, my mum supporting her from behind. Very quickly, Mum's arthritic arms gave out on her. With a groan she passed Megan over to Emily, who twirled her around and around. Megan squealed and giggled and squealed again.

My heart performed a flip as I watched them, but then I noticed Josh, who was hanging back on the drive. 'Come and say hello, Josh,' I said gently, with a nod of my head. He trudged forward shyly, keeping his eyes down on his over-large trainers.

'And here's Joshy,' my mum said warmly, drawing him into the fold. Megan looked at him, suddenly serious.

'We call him Dude,' Jamie said.

'Jewd,' Megan attempted and then laughed.

Josh grinned.

Megan was hyper for the rest of the day. She kept running from one toy box to another, picking things up, giving them a kiss and then abandoning them for something else. She broke her heart at bedtime though, crying piteously every time I attempted to leave her room. I had moved my own bed into the room that was intended as a dining room, and several times I took her down to show her where I'd be sleeping. She seemed to find it comforting to know exactly where I'd be.

It was weeks before she trusted me enough to let me out of her sight. In many ways, she was a different little girl to the one I'd moved on. Every morning she'd ask what we were doing for the day, her face a picture of anguish if I told her we were going to visit friends or fellow foster carers. She tensed whenever I got her shoes and coat out. 'No! Want stay here!' she'd cry.

Her fears were compounded in March, when Josh moved into a long-term placement. Josh's social worker had asked me to prepare an inventory of his belongings, so the day before the move I itemised everything; each piece of clothing, and all the bits and pieces we had bought for him in the last few weeks. It was a process that every foster carer was supposed to go through every time a child joined and then left them for a new placement, or to return home, so that any disputes over missing items could be avoided. Not every social worker insisted on it being done, but Josh's social worker had been stung once before, a parent insisting that their son had taken a Wii console and a PSP with them when they moved into foster care. Without an inventory to refer to it was difficult to prove otherwise, and the local authority ended up having to replace the 'missing' items.

Naturally, Josh was nervous about the move, and as he helped me go through his things, he grew gloomy and tearful. Megan picked up on his distress, and both of them shadowed me for the rest of the day, even when I went to visit the bathroom. Sitting side by side, they waited anxiously outside the door for me to emerge.

When Megan saw Josh's suitcases in the hall she ran off to hide under the table. It took ages to coax her out and when she did, I wasn't quite sure how far I should go in reassuring her that she wasn't about to leave as well.

I was reluctant to make any promises for fear of undermining her faith in adults if she were to have to leave us again. By April, though, I began to feel a lot more confident that Megan was here to stay. My assessing social worker assured me that my application to adopt was being fast-tracked, and barring the unearthing of shocking secrets from my past or unexpected criminal convictions, she couldn't imagine anything going wrong.

Around the middle of the month I ordered some books from Amazon that were written especially for adopted children. We read them together, and one, *I Wished for You* by Marianne Richmond, became one of Megan's firm favourites. She also loved *I Promise I'll Find You* by Heather Ward, a story about a parent who searches the world for her lost child. The first time I read it to her, she climbed off my lap and looked at me askance. 'Mummy no come back for long time.'

I brushed her fringe back from her forehead. 'Listen to me, sweetie. You don't have to worry. You're not going anywhere else ever again. You're staying right here with Rosie and Emily and Jamie, forever and ever.'

She still looked dubious. 'Ever and ever?'

I smiled and kissed her head. 'Yes, absolutely. You're going to be Megan Lewis, my daughter. I love you very much, and you're going to be part of the family forever.'

She tilted her head to one side, considering. 'How long is forever?'

Chapter Forty-Six

One morning in April, when Megan had been back living with us for two months, the doorbell rang unexpectedly.

Still terrified that someone was going to take her away without a moment's notice, Megan threw herself at me and wrapped her arms tightly around my neck. With her balanced on my hip, I walked through the hall, all the while trying to comfort her with low, soothing words.

When I opened the door though, my breath caught in my throat. Megan cried out, digging her nails into the skin on my neck. 'It's all right, Megan, it's all right,' I said, hardly able to believe that there, standing on the doorstep with his old rucksack thrown over his shoulder, was Des. Megan's vice-like grip relaxed, but only slightly. Her cheek was still pressed tightly against mine.

'Rosie,' Des said simply, as if turning up out of the blue after two years of absence was the most natural thing in the world. I stared at him, frowning. Believing that he was still working in the States, I couldn't quite process it was him. But it wasn't only that. His hair was different as well. When he left it had been wildly curly, untamed and brushing his shoulders. It was shorter now, falling in neat soft waves around his face. His brow furrowed. 'Have you's company? Is it a bad time?'

Megan brought me to my senses. Having realised that she was safe, she wriggled out of my arms and stepped hesitantly forward. Testing the water, she reached out and patted Des's leg. 'Hey, sweetheart,' he whispered softly. Gazing up, she gave him a shy smile.

I shook my head. 'No, sorry, it's not a bad time at all. I'm just surprised to see you.' Apart from the odd postcard addressed to The Lewis Family, we had barely heard anything from him since he left.

Des picked Megan up and then wobbled on his feet, pretending to buckle under the weight. 'Gee, wee lassie. I can't believe how big you are.' She looked delighted at that and crowed a loud laugh.

'We've got some news, Des.'

Megan was patting his head with both hands. 'I know your news,' he said, angling his head and throwing me a knowing smile through the gap in her arms. Her fingers began to roam over his craggy face, and then she began familiarising herself with his nostrils. Des made a growling noise and she snatched her hands away, giggling.

'How do you know?'

A smile touched his lips and he raised his eyebrows. 'I have my sources, Mrs Lewis. You donae think I'd go away without keeping tabs on my favourite foster carer, do you?

Now, are you's going to leave me standing on the step all day or are you's going to make me a cup of tea?'

My eyes brimmed with tears. I dabbed my face on my sleeve, smiled, and stood aside to let him in.

Epilogue

Several weekend courses, Disclosure and Barring Service and solvency checks, interviews with friends and family, and employment references followed, along with some daft and wildly inappropriate questions. I still fail to see the relevance of whether or not I have friends that are Christian (and I'm not sure what the correct answer should be either), but thankfully the social worker assigned to assessing me as an adopter approved my application, and the 20 or so professionals making up the adoption panel agreed with the decision.

Peggy had provided a glowing reference, as well as the manager of Bright Heights fostering agency and all of the social workers of my past placements.

Even after attending the panel, I still couldn't bring myself to believe that Megan was finally going to be ours. As the weeks passed she began to relax, but my own fears of separation lingered.

And so it was that on a grey and overcast day in June 2014, with Megan's celebration hearing scheduled for 10 o'clock, I woke with my heart thumping high up in my chest. In reality, the hearing was merely for show; the formalities had taken place behind closed doors weeks earlier, but I could still hardly speak on the journey to the city centre, although I doubted that anyone else noticed. Emily, who was thrilled by the idea of going to court, had barely drawn breath since we left the house. Jamie, initially disgruntled at having to wear a suit, had eventually stopped rolling his shoulders and grimacing, pleased at having an excuse for a day off school.

The grey clouds were beginning to break up as we approached the stone building housing the Family and Magistrates' Court. We climbed the front steps with hands intertwined, all of us falling silent as we passed through the ornately carved wooden doors. As a security guard checked through our bags, Megan began singing an indecipherable song and skipping through the stone arches. The guard smiled broadly. 'Enjoy your day,' he said, sensing, I suspect, that ours wasn't a case of repossession or divorce.

An usher accompanied us to courtroom 19, telling us what to expect from the hearing. 'Should the judge wear his ceremonial dress?' she asked, as we approached a set of stairs. 'It's nice for the photographs, but some little ones are a bit daunted by the sight of the gown and wig.'

Megan powered away from me and stamped up each stair, shouting, 'Boom, boom, boom!' with every step. I turned and gave a wry smile to the usher.

She grinned. 'I'm guessing she'll be fine.'

Veronica was already waiting in the upstairs foyer when we got there. She got to her feet to greet us. 'It all worked out in the end,' she said warmly, and as she shook my hand I got the impression that she meant it.

Inside the wood-panelled chamber, my mind ran over the last three years; the hopes raised and then dashed. It was hard to believe that Megan was finally part of our family, her status as my daughter sealed in law. My nerves jangled when the usher asked us all to rise. Megan, fidgeting on the bench beside me, stilled as the judge made his entrance. She stared at him, her mouth falling open.

She was still spellbound as he made his opening speech, talking about the value of being part of a loving family and the lifelong commitment that adoption entailed. 'What that man got on his head?' she asked, before he'd finished speaking.

I shushed her, but the judge turned to Megan, his eyes twinkling. 'This is a special wig that judges wear. And I can see you're wearing a special dress as well. You look very smart.'

Megan looked down at herself and then back at the judge. 'Mummy bought it me. I not allowed to eat choc choc in it though,' she added solemnly. The judge chuckled, and all of the ushers laughed as well.

'Excellent. Well, you seem like a very happy little girl to me, wouldn't you say so, Mummy?'

He was smiling warmly and I felt choked when I answered. 'She's wonderfully happy, sir. And so are we.'

Despite his formal attire, the judge was friendly and approachable. He smiled broadly in all the photographs, and even allowed Megan to sit in his grand chair for one of them. Before leaving the courtroom, he shook our hands, presented Megan with a certificate and wished us a very happy future together.

Outside on the street, Des stood waiting for us. Behind him, the sun finally emerged from behind the clouds.

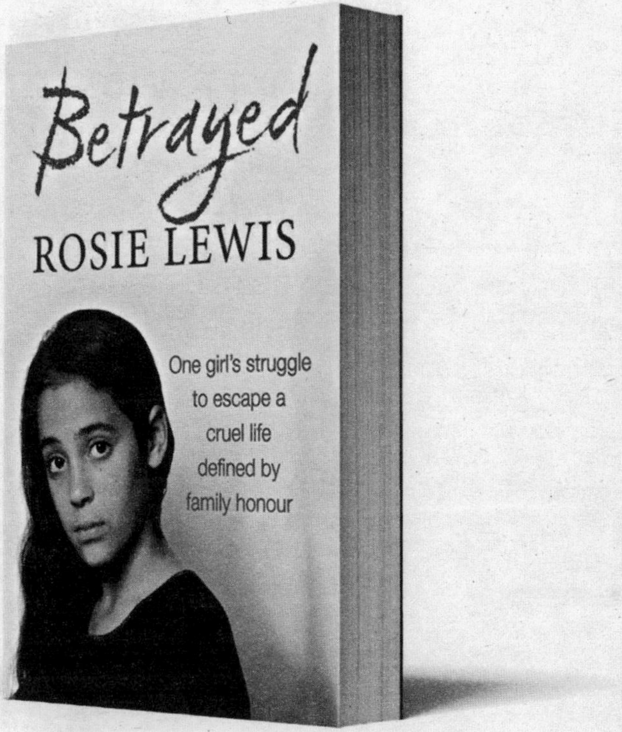

The struggle to escape a life defined by family honour

With Rosie's support, 13-year-old Zadie gradually begins to settle into her new surroundings. But loyalty to her relatives and fear of bringing shame on her family keeps preventing Zadie from confessing the horrifying truth about her past. Will Rosie be able to persuade her to open up in time?

BETRAYED

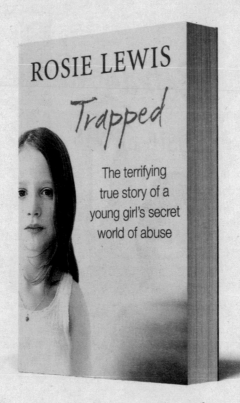

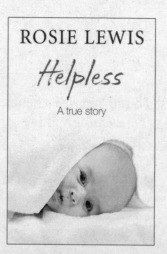

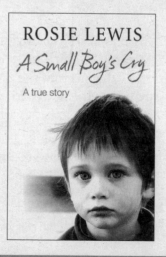

Found beneath a bench, seemingly alone

Angell comes into the home and heart of foster carer Rosie Lewis. Will Angell be destined to spend the rest of her childhood in care or will her mother return for her?

TWO MORE SLEEPS

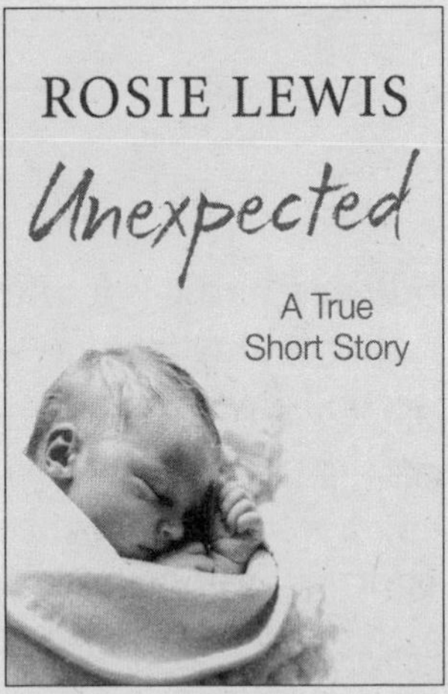

Ellen is so shocked by the sudden birth of her baby girl that she abandons the newborn in hospital

Rosie struggles to understand how anyone can treat a baby in this way, but with time she begins to see the dark secret Ellen is hiding.

UNEXPECTED